QUESTIONING POLITICS:

FIVE ESSENTIAL QUERIES FOR BELIEVERS TO ASK AND ANSWER

David W. Hall

The Covenant Foundation
© 2011

DAVID W. HALL

Table of Contents

Introduction

The Problem in 1992 and Why this work is still needed

I had been up much of the night watching presidential election returns in November 1992. Third party candidate Ross Perot, along with a moderate Republican, coupled with a charismatic "New Democrat" candidate all worked to reward President William Clinton with his first of two terms. As a pastor, however, I was most stunned when I arrived at our church's Wednesday night prayer meeting the following day. The saints could hardly pray—certainly could not be joyful always. They were shocked, despondent, defeated, and fairly clueless. Following eight years of Ronald Reagan's presidency—often considered a Golden age by some—and four years under President George H. W. Bush, our evangelical church was crushed and rudderless.

For years, they had marched in pro-life events, sent postcards to representatives, worked phone banks, and distributed Voters Guides from various religious groups. And after 12 years of GOP rule, few of their values had been adopted, except in abstract ways, and the gains seemed flimsy. Within days, by executive orders policies like "Don't Ask, Don't Tell" were instituted and the lifting of abortion curbs were razed. In view of such shifting political sands, many Christians would ask: "Where did we go wrong?" "Is our country hopelessly doomed?" and "Can America survive a liberal?"

My questions, however, were more immediate. Seizing the moment for reflection, I needed to ask, "What has the church been doing that has led us to be so reactive to one election?" and "What have we done right or wrong?" and "How should we disciple to avoid the defeatism so palpable in that prayer room that night?" "How, in short, could we be more faithful?"

That led me to almost twenty years of discussion, study, and biblical reflection on politics and government. To be sure, I am no expert, but this work seeks to draw from the mind of Another expert, who has far more insight than the combination of the best of our ancients and our contemporaries.

Pre-Sets

Let me candidly state my conclusion from the outset: Should the Christian community advance in its biblical application in matters of state for 30-40 years, we would at best return to the political maturity of the common citizen in the 1750s. Typical statements by James Madison, Patrick Henry, and other founding fathers of America reveal how stable and informed their political thinking was. Consider, for example, not only that Madison's statement below was written for public consumption (in the popular press), but moreover its sensitivity toward the Christian teaching about human sinfulness.

> Ambition must be made to counteract ambition. The interest of the man must be connected with the constitutional rights of the place. It may be a reflection on human nature, that such devices should be necessary to control the abuses of government. But what is government itself, but the greatest of all reflections on human nature? If men were angels, no government would be necessary. If angels were to govern men, neither external nor internal controls on government would be necessary. (*The Federalist (#51) Papers*; interestingly, John Calvin wrote almost verbatim two centuries earlier in his commentary on *Galatians*[1])

---

[1] John Calvin, *Sermons on Galatians* (Edinburgh: Banner of Truth Trust, 1996),

This kind and depth of thinking epitomized the fruition of previous centuries' application of Scripture to the nature and role of government. It is still an opportune moment to reinvent government to be sure. However, pensive citizens might prefer to re-model politics following the *ethos* of limited government as such earlier constitutionalists envisioned, rather than pine after utopianism's hope.

Two important points need to be acknowledged. *First*, the American constitution (1789) did not spring into existence like Athena, immediately from the forehead of Zeus. Neither was it an exact copy of other existing constitutions. There were few, if any, models for the colonists to follow. They started from scratch in the sense that they inherited little tradition and no sitting monarchy; thus allowing a bold experiment. The U. S. constitution, however, did have predecessors. As the constitutional fathers met in Philadelphia, they bore the sure impress of previous thinkers.

While the uniqueness of this constitution must be appreciated, a *second* point to grant is that the American founding fathers had hundreds of years of previous theology from which to draw. And draw on it they did; particularly the theology of the 200 years prior to 1789. The U. S. constitution has discernible traces of the ideas of Bucer, Calvin, Beza, Knox, Althusius and others—more theologians than many anticipate. It is almost as if the teachings of those theologians had so saturated culture that even the common man understood and embraced that world view. Consequently, some go so far as to allude to Calvin as the ideological Father of the American Republic.

What one sees in the U. S. constitution is the incarnation of Medieval and Reformation principles that were given free and unhindered implementation for the first time. This unique constitution both rests upon the shoulders of those who have gone before and continues to be beneficial. A Reformation theology of the state formed much of the intellectual matrix prior to the U. S. constitution; it shows. Should we hope to get back to that pinnacle,

---

313.

or progress beyond that point, we must grasp anew the underlying theology of the state.

I will consider this short work a successful tool if it provides a springboard for discussions of faith and politics from a Christian perspective. It will be an advance if we question some of the prevailing notions. If somehow, Christian thought about governmental matters can be anchored to biblical conclusions, and also be refined by historical and systematic theological factors, then hopefully one can at least avoid many of the mistakes of the past. Indeed, if most Christians could simply avoid the errors of the past and formulate matters of state avoiding those mis-steps, most of us would be better off.

One is tempted to ask in Reaganesque fashion, "Are you better off now than you were 4(000) years ago?" Have modern governments really improved over ancient systems of government? Under modern governments, some citizens receive more benefits, and there have definitely been technological improvements in information systems. However, if all things are considered, can one conclude with certainty that citizens are more free, less hindered by the interests of politicians, more moral, and more able to pursue godly interests with stability than in the past? Or have some governments actually been de-evolutionary, regressive overall rather than progressive? The answers contained in this discussion may surprise, particularly as some re-consider the appropriate size and scope of the state.

No volume of this sort can answer every political issue or resolve every hypothetical question that might be raised. However, evangelicals have long needed a short but thorough theology of the state. Although we'll not cover every single verse in Scripture, I will seek to bring in as many as possible in a short span. Indeed, God's Word has much to say on matters of politics. This book is self-consciously limited, however, by another important fact: This theology of the state seeks to limit itself to the revelation of the mind of God. While Holy Scripture is a perfectly reliable guide for subjects on which it informs, there are matters about which it does not inform. Thus, there are certain facts, aspects, and issues that are not explicitly treated in Scripture. In keeping with the belief that God revealed all that is necessary for life and godliness (2 Pet. 1:3), accordingly, lower status and lesser attention is given to those questions that are not addressed by the canon of Scripture.

One of the first and most important ideas is treated below. We begin by understanding that God has many governments to order society—not merely one.

First Principle: God gives plural [corporate] governments, not just one

God has created Spheres at least three separate and legitimate spheres of corporate government: the family, the church, and the civil government.[2] The family was chartered by God before the entrance of sin into the world and is charged to cultivate and order matters of the home. It should be respected and unhindered. The family is to care for all that God assigns to it, without interference from any other governing sphere.

The church is a society also created and ordained by God. It, too, was decreed prior to the Fall of mankind. All redeemed believers are in the church; and the church is governed by the principles and hierarchies of Scripture. It is to spread the gospel, disciple members, provide worship, and enjoy the sacraments. The church should not seek to do the job of the family, nor the state. And it should be respected and supported by both.

The civil state is designed by God to preserve order and keep citizens safe. It is not chartered as an overtly religious institution, although it is derived from the Creator. The state should not seek to do the work of other spheres, but is essential to order in a fallen society. Most commentators agree that the state was created to deal with sinful conditions.

In scripture, the family is symbolized by the rod; the church by the keys, and the state by the sword. Each is a valid government,

---

[2] Some commentators describe self-government, or personal responsibility, as the first sphere of government. As crucial and essential as that doubtlessly is, we are speaking of corporate spheres of government.

and neither is to interfere with the duty of the others. Each of these valid spheres are unique and essential.

As one understands this beginning division of labor, it helps to embrace the fact that God plans to use many different agencies in this world. All things are not committed to a single monopolistic government.

This initial concept helps understand and address this important question: Where does the responsibility lie? To whom is this given? A clear answer to that question will provide guidance for more political questions than one imagines.

With the loss of the right to prayer in schools (1963) and the legalization of abortion (1973), American Christians slowly realized that the state was no longer protecting values that once were assumed to be guaranteed. By the late 1970s, Francis Schaeffer warned that any state devoid of absolutes would inevitably clash with the religious absolutes held by believers: "No totalitarian authority nor authoritarian state can tolerate those who have an absolute by which to judge that state and its actions."[3] During the 1980s, the march of secularism made steady advances. In the early 1980s, groups like Jerry Falwell's *Moral Majority* and Pat Robertson's *700 Club* took notice of these trends as did many others. Meanwhile, Christian Reconstructionists arose, calling for a return to biblical prescriptions for the government. In the late 1980s, several attempts were made to articulate how Christians should view the role of Government.[4] It was almost as if the Christian church had been caught off guard; and while under siege, it hastily thrust an

---

[3] Francis Schaeffer, *How Should We Then Live, The Complete Works of Francis A. Schaeffer* (Westchester, IL: Crossway, 1982), 5: 88.

[4] For example, cf. John Eidsmoe's *God and Caesar* (Westchester, IL: Crossway, 1984); Gary DeMar and George Grant's *God and Government* (Atlanta: American Vision, 1986); George Grant's, *The Changing of the Guard* (orig. 1987, and republished Chicago: Moody, 1995); Michael Cromartie's *Disciples and Democracy* (Washington, DC: Ethics and Public Policy Center, 1994); Chuck Colson's *Kingdoms in Conflict* (Grand Rapids: Zondervan, 1991); Rousas Rushdoony's *Christianity and the State* (Vallecito, CA: Ross House Books, 1986); and Doug Bandow's *Beyond Good Intentions* (Wheaton: Crossway, 1988). Cf also Francis Schaeffer's *A Christian Manifesto* (Crossway, 1981).

army into battle, but in 1992 unfortunately failed to understand the terms of engagement or the marching orders.

Is the situation very different 20 years later? Is progress being made? Will it be made if we fail to question the politics around us? Christians entered the political theaters *en masse*, mainly out of a sense of impending doom or urgent necessity. Resulting actions have not always been as biblically researched or grounded as other areas of Christian living. It is high time that Christians questioned some of the politics around us; and also came up with more durable answers.

The Vacuum

Few systematic biblical treatments of this important area of life have been available. When Francis Schaeffer was asked to recommend a sound biblical treatise on government in the 1970s, more often than not, all he could commend was an obscure (and at that time out of print) seventeenth century work with a Latin title: *Lex Rex* by Samuel Rutherford. Schaeffer was astute to commend such a solid work, but few of his audience could ever find—much less persevere through—this sturdy and worthwhile book.[5] Rutherford's book did state the roles of the rulers to the revealed law of God, but it was concerned with many issues that seemed impertinent to democratic society.

When pressed to produce other previous works on this subject, materials were scarce. With a paucity of prior information, evangelicals hastily composed literature with an obvious sense of urgency. Often such books were based either on an individual's experience, expertise in politics (not necessarily biblically examined), or the preoccupation with a single predominating issue. For example, one can read autobiographies of Christians who have

---

[5] Fortunately, it was re-published in 1984 by Sprinkle Publications (Harrisonburg, VA) for the first time in nearly two centuries. Now this classic volume is available at Amazon.com or at http://www.constitution.org/sr/lexrex.htm. Also see John Coffey's 2002 *Politics, Religion and the British Revolutions: The Mind of Samuel Rutherford* (Cambridge University Press).

been involved in politics (Chuck Colson, Jimmy Carter, George W. Bush, or almost any presidential candidate). Moreover, books on single issues (e.g., abortion, just war, economics) are readily available. However, most of these fail to be comprehensive and risk imbalance as they focus on one issue above others.

Three additional reasons accentuate the need for a work of this type. *First*, as already intimated, more Bible-believing Christians in the USA have become involved in politics since 1975 than in any time in recent memory. The only other close rivals for evangelical insurgence were the various reform movements of the nineteenth century. Unfortunately, however, this surge of activism has not always been based on sound and systematic biblical teaching. Expecting that matters of government will continue in importance in the next decades, evangelicals will do well to systematically explore some of these concepts before the next idea wars commence.

Second, concerns for biblical fidelity in matters of state call for an ongoing critique of present matters. The West in the past half century has been fairly dominated by liberal or leftist trends. Evangelicals have become more vigilant and effective of late to critique these. Suppose, however, that a conservative or rightist trend were to dominate the next half century. Might not those secular conservatives incline toward excess as well as secular liberals? In order to provide balance, the scriptural revelation must be adhered to, lest Christians become buffeted by the prevailing winds of culture. It is possible for political movements to trend in culturally conservative directions, but not be in accord with the full range of biblical teaching. The right can be as wrong as the left. This attempted "true mean" study seeks to avoid unbelieving conservatism merely as a reaction to secular liberalism. At times it seems as though if evangelicals could remake society, they would merely parrot the secular conservative causes of the day.[6] We hope for a more sound and enduring basis.

---

[6] For example, to elevate approval of Star Wars missile defense programs to a level of some 'biblical scorecards' may be a case of championing a conservative cause that the Christian may not necessarily be obliged to advocate. National defense is needed, but specific programmatic means to that end may not have

Third, most systematic theology books offer little or no detailed teaching on this subject. The formulation of matters of state in most classic theological books is a noticeable lacuna. There is much on most subjects in such standard theological texts (e.g., Berkhof, Calvin, Luther, Pieper, Hodge, Buswell, Bavinck, Dabney, Turretin, Erickson, Grudem[7]). However, one can hardly find systematic biblical reference to a theology of the state. Few resources above an experiential basis are available. Popular and experiential approaches have therefore, by default, reigned in this area.

For example, if the average Christian leader wishes to consult a theology of the state, one could find the following from classic texts:

Theologian	Total pages	Theology of the State	Percentage
Hodge	2,260	0	(0%)
Dabney	887	10	(1%)
Buswell	983	10	(1%)
Shedd	803	0	(0%)
Berkhof	740	0	(0%)
Bavinck	568	0	(0%)
Calvin	1,521	36	(2%)
Total	**7,762**	**56**	**(0.7%)**

Less than one percent of the leading systematic theology texts address a matter which now consumes far more than one percent of the average Christian's interest. More than half of that comes from a single theologian (Calvin). In contrast, some recent popular works devote hundreds of pages to various aspects of the state. However, not all Christians agree with those views, and the amount of attention given to this area often indicates a preoccupation which betrays that some discussions may be reactionary or imbalanced. While it is commendable that some from various camps of belief are

---

biblical support.

[7] Thankfully, in late 2010, Wayne Grudem released a very comprehensive treatise, entitled *Politics According to the Bible* (Grand Rapids: Zondervan, 2010).

finally giving massive attention to matters of government, it is imperative that such endeavors preserve a sense of proportion.

Bible-believing Christians need a balanced and systematic discussion of matters of state. We should have had such a resource long ago, but with the press of other concerns, the church has not always articulated its views on subjects until after the fact. The honest purpose of what is contained herein is simply to exhibit biblical guidance on the intersection of faith and politics. Other agendas are not intended.

Let me hasten to make a few disclaimers. This approach is not intended to be a partisan tract. It is neither commissioned by, sponsored by, nor affiliated with any existing political party. I am aware that, for example, in the last 5-6 presidential elections, the vast majority of self-identified evangelical Christians supported the Republican candidate. However, even the most ardent Republican evangelical would not claim that the GOP has exclusive theological priority in the Kingdom of God. This biblical study is above present party affiliation and, by the nature of the case, must be. It attempts to put forth eternal and enduring principles which Christians in any age—past or future—could endorse. This book is not a manifesto for a partisan rally.

To illustrate our desire, neither is this discussion intended to be applicable to only one period of history. It is not a tractate written only for the early twenty-first century. Nor is it designed only for Americans or western democracies, although admittedly that is our location. The biblical teaching on the role of the state transcends nations and eras. If we do identify some of God's eternal principles on these matters, then they should be equally applicable in 1200 BC, AD 1200, or AD 2200 (should the Lord tarry). Frequently, I have asked myself (and other counselors along the way): "Is my discussion hopelessly biased by our present western democratic location? Am I faithfully interpreting biblical truth such that it will still be true in 1,000 years? Was it true 1,000 years ago?" We are not interested in producing a time-laden discussion that, like many others, will be dated by the next election cycle or in the next decade.

Our focus is on lasting principles that will guide Christians for all times.

We believe that biblical teaching on the role of the state has no more changed than Christian teaching on human sinfulness, sanctification, salvation by grace, or the doctrine of the Holy Spirit. If we rightly interpret Scripture—on this or any other subject—then such conclusions ought to be true for more ages than our own. If not, then we may rightly question whether or not we have interpreted Scripture correctly.

Second Principle: The Knowledge Basis of Information

Philosophers are fond of dwelling on epistemology—the study of the basis for knowledge. A structure is only as sound as its foundation. The remainder of this book is founded on a simple premise: *God who created the state has also revealed how it should operate.* Those who believe the formulations below will also observe the same logic in our approach:

God who created the human body	knows best how it works and its limitations;
God who created the family	knows best how it works and its limitations;
God who created the church	knows best how it works and its limitations;
God who created economics	knows best how it works and its limitations.

The Creator of the state *knows best how it works and its limitations.* This discussion is, thus, from an explicitly and unambiguously religious viewpoint. The knowledge basis of this discussion will be the canonical Scripture. We will be both limited by and dependent on that in the subsequent formulations. We realize, of course, that some will not agree with our foundation, but surely all will agree that we can question prevailing political customs in search of improving our public square.

Among others, Don Eberly noted how essential religious values are for the state: "A country in which there is no transcendent foundation for law, politics, economics and society is a disordered and potentially dangerous place. If utilitarianism, not religious and ethical values, guides our conduct, then might makes right. In the policy and management sciences, this philosophy produced a wholly mechanistic and material view of man."[8]

Similarly, Gertrude Himmelfarb has argued that moral concerns have been inextricably interwoven with public policy. Citing the British Victorians, Himmelfarb concludes: "The divorce of social policy from moral principles—the de-moralization of social policy—also reflects the spirit of relativism that is so pervasive in our time. . . . We have tried the 'value-free' social policies and they do not work. . . . And having made the most determined effort to devise social policies that are 'value-free,' that do not stigmatize relief-recipients or oblige them to behave morally . . . we find that these policies demoralize and pauperize their intended beneficiaries."[9]

It should soon be admitted (or discovered) that any and all governmental systems are based on pre-conceived values. In fact, no governmental program is isolated from its underlying world view. A philosophical world view is the interpretive matrix for all these studies; ours as well. Recognition of that from the outset is imperative.

Former Education Secretary William J. Bennett went so far as to say that, "The theological dimension is needed both for interpreting and solving present-day problems in human society. . . . If there is no ultimate truth to guide and direct political activity, then ideas and convictions can easily be manipulated for reasons of power. As history demonstrates, a democracy without values turns into open or thinly disguised totalitarianism."[10]

---

[8] Don Eberly, "Even Newt Can't Save Us," *The Wall Street Journal*, Feb. 3, 1995, p. A12. He continues: "The entire central, top-down, rule-driven administrative state designed on this premise is now being thrown off, not simply because of its grotesque inefficiencies, but because it miniaturizes man. In ethics, a system based on sensation regards sensory happiness, pleasure and comfort as the supreme value. The result is moral relativism and cultural nihilism."

[9] Gertrude Himmelfarb, "Re-Moralizing America," *The Wall Street Journal*, Feb. 7, 1995, p. A22.

[10] William J. Bennett, *The De-Valuing of America* (New York: Summit Books, 1992), 208.

The point is: All politics are not merely local (as Speaker of the House, Tip O'Neill, was fond of saying); all politics are also theological. Views of the state and its limitations are inescapably rooted in a world view and in practical consequence. If either fails, so will the epiphenomena. A certain amount of theology, or appeal to ultimate principles taken on faith, is unavoidable in formulating political views.

M. Stanton Evans has written persuasively about this "theological determinism" and the priority of biblical religion to shape the good society.

> When religious value is denied in the realm of spirit, but reasserted in the secular order, dominion over every facet of life converges in a single center; the political regime becomes both church and state, and claims authority over faith and conscience. It is this crushing, all-pervasive assertion of power over every aspect of existence, without exception or reserve, that is the truly distinguishing feature of the totalitarian movements. It is what makes totalitarianism 'total'. . . pagan cultures united religious and secular functions in the state, thereby precluding the idea of limits on its power, foreclosing the notion of any higher loyalty, denying refuge to the spirit. Judaism and Christianity opened the door to a different world, in which the ideas and practices of freedom could develop. Modern neopaganism has moved to close that door again, in even more decisive fashion.[11]

It might even be helpful, albeit unconventional, to ask this question: which religions help to enhance political culture? For example, Eastern religions (including the New Age movement) have provided few political advances throughout history. Many countries identified with Hinduism and Buddhism are associated with political tyranny, instability, and corruption. Nearly half the world's population (in China, Japan, and India) live under governmental structures which are incompatible with the best biblical applications to government. A large measure of socialism is present in these

---

[11] M. Stanton Evans, *The Theme is Freedom* (Washington, DC: Regnery, 1994), 121.

societies. Further, their sacred texts—being largely preoccupied with the mystical or personal—have little instruction on the role of government in general or the civil state's role in particular. Thus, religious instruction from the Eastern religions offers little material help. Nor should it be expected that religions that are largely gnostic will provide much guidance on matters as mundane as government. A philosophical bias in most Eastern religions restricts their value in matters of state.

Eastern Orthodox churches also have limited information on this subject. While the former Soviet Union was once a mainstay of Christian orthodoxy, over the past century the powerful atheistic state claimed a total dominance over the state church. The Russian Orthodox church provided little resistance to the Bolshevik revolution; except for a vital underground church, the largest of the Orthodox churches proved lacking in matters of statecraft.

The animistic African religions fail to provide much information on the structure of government, their own instabilities perhaps the strongest argument against their pedagogical value. Moreover, the Islamic countries have, until recently, been models of disorganization and of the reign of caprice or tribalism. Of late, the modern Islamic republics have grown in power, but not so much due to their theories of government as due to their location near valuable natural resources. Further, these various sheikdoms have been exemplars of the rule by petty fiefs—often arbitrary, brutal, and unstable.

Indeed, it is difficult to dispute that for the past 500 years the clear leaders in political construct have been those western nations that were earlier and traditionally based on Christian values. The leaders in developing working democracies have been the countries of western Europe and America. Perhaps earlier theorists were not so mistaken when they identified a correlation between Protestant faith and certain political values which led to developing healthy societies.

The three major theologies of the West have been Judaism, Catholicism, and Protestantism. All three bring important contributions to the questions we will consider. Judaism will be well represented by the Old Testament (hereafter, OT) studies. Roman Catholicism has a long tradition of views of the state, most of which is compatible with other Protestant and Jewish ideas. And the Protestant tradition claims to be the leader in returning self-rule to many nations. While not agreeing in certain theological areas, this study will seek to elucidate areas of commonality among these three.

The Importance of History as Context

Another beginning question is this: Are we limited only to the best wisdom on our own generation? Can there be, in other words, no broader sources of political wisdom than our own time and place? In mature reflection on government, history is a stalwart assistant as a corroborating guide. One assumption is that over even large periods of time, the human condition and social solutions are basically constant. Therefore, it is believed that one is unwise to fail to benefit from what has successfully worked in other eras.

Strikingly similar political, social and environmental dynamics were present early on in the OT. Thus our situations are not really novel. Though sobering, it is helpful to realize that in many respects the problems and foundational dynamics have barely changed over time. The course of wisdom requires us to be reticent to endorse political proposals that begin by defining the challenges as totally unique, non-normal, or without parallel. To esteem our own exigencies as categorically unique or a "crisis," is either a by-product of inordinate fear or *hubris*, and leads to a skewed perspective that tends to diminish rational solutions in deference to the perceived magnitude of the "crisis." By the time of Abraham (ca. 2000 BC), the following socio-political dynamics were already present:

* difficulty of labor to provide necessities for living (Gen. 3:18-19)
* fratricide (Gen. 4:8)
* violent homicide (Gen. 4:23)
* moral wickedness (Gen. 6:5 and 8:20)
* ecological disaster (Gen. 7-9)

* sexual sin (Gen. 9:22)
* tribal (gang?) warfare (Gen. 10:8-9)
* infertility (Sarah)
* competition for income (Gen. 13:8-9)
* consequences stemming from military conquests (Gen. 14)
* ethnic hostility (Gen. 16:12)
* homosexuality (Gen. 19:5)
* family alienation (Gen. 21:8 ff.).

Thus with what sounds like the findings of causes of societal ill from a modern Commission, we will want to be careful before pronouncing that we are in a completely new or unique situation. Such claims will have to be scrutinized and judged by the principle enunciated by Solomon that, "There is nothing new under the sun" (Eccl. 1:9-11; 3:15).[12] That being the case, the plethora of problems takes on a different cast than when one is led to believe that solutions must be created *de novo*. If the problems and dynamics of the human *polis* are largely static, then we are afforded a calmer opportunity to assess solutions with more reason and balance than if we are impetuously required to create a state without the larger principles given by the great Creator of society. One of the aspects of this perspective is that both problems and solutions will be normatively similar over time.[13] Certainly there is external change in societies, but that is not to say that the root problems or remedial reforms have changed substantially. Once again, an aged set of norms may be more helpful than the latest studies, particularly if such modernity-biased studies are flawed at the outset with an ignorance of historical similarities.

---

[12] Thomas Sowell, *The Vision of the Anointed* (New York: Basic Books, 1995), 6-9 provides an excellent aetiology of modern failures to remedy manufactured crises.

[13] As this work was being written, much of the political discussion was consumed with what might happen if leaders did not agree on a forthcoming budget. With teeming predictions of an impending governmental train wreck, however, one would have been well-served to recall that in the decade of the 1980s, seven out of ten years saw such train wrecks—all apparently without providing any incentive toward actual budget reductions.

Christians view matters of state as important. This study avoids government-bashing and criticism of those involved in the political realm. One cannot argue from Scripture that either government *per se*, or politics as a calling, is inherently wrong or evil. In fact, this whole arena of human activity is treated with high regard as an object of God's design. John Calvin even referred to political governors as "vicars" of Christ—an exalted title, to be sure. If God is the Designer of the state, then it should be ordered in keeping with that design that is found most perfectly in the inspired Scripture. The enduring challenge is to put government in its proper place.

We will often ask questions about prevailing, unexamined assumptions. And to answer many of those with a more enduring set of information, especially if revealed from an omniscient Source, can hardly be wrong.

Chapter 1

The Origin and Divine Plan for GovernmentS (Plural): Or Is Politics All There Is?

OT Foundations: Light from the Torah

To look around at various news reports and to listen to many speakers today, one would construe that political solutions must be forthcoming or else we face certain catastrophe. Some from state houses act as though only elected officials can cure problems. Some within churches act as though only if a change in governors occurs can Christianity continue. A contrarian voice may occasionally ask in a forum: Is politics all there is? Or can politics fix our greatest ills? Might there not be many non-political solutions that should be considered? Such radical questioning is in order, and there is light from the ancient Torah on many more matters than some may assume.

The opening chapters of Genesis raise the major themes that are still subject to discussion today.[14] The first chapter of Scripture even

---

[14] Instead of a method that states systematic conclusions and then arranges material accordingly, the retracing of the canonical unfolding honors the purpose of God to gradually reveal his will. Believing that God is a "God of order" (1 Cor.

provides a basic pattern for matters of government, albeit indirectly, as well as a denial to the expectation that all matters may be politically solved. Genesis 1:16 states that God created the two major lights (the sun and the moon), which are evident from earth. Those created luminaries were designed to "rule" over the day or the night; and importantly, not vice-versa. Each "light" was designed to rule over a limited jurisdiction. Thus, early on in creation one may observe that God creates but then delegates certain prerogatives to his creation. That is true for government—familial, civil, or ecclesiastical. The state as a human agency for organization is created by God, and is to be maintained in keeping with his design. A state may lawfully acknowledge that it is not *de novo*, and still maintain its prerogatives to govern. Governance, by nature, is delegated from the Creator. The roles within governments, therefore, are not purely human, nor created by the will of man. Most perfectly, any system that rules will do so sensitive to its status as created, and not confuse itself with, nor usurp, the prerogatives of its Creator. On the other extreme, states which do not acknowledge their status as created may be prone to call on their subjects to treat the state (or some other created object—Rom. 1:21-26) as divine.

Later in Genesis 1, the idea of "dominion" validates human government as a legitimate activity as long as it is confined to its proper creaturely role. Genesis 1:26, 28 contain divine commands for humans to "rule" over certain areas. The specified areas in this case are over animal life and "over every living creature that moves on the ground." Psalm 8:6 also affirms that God established humans to be "ruler[s] over the works of [God's] hands." Often referred to as the "cultural mandate," these commands certainly include governmental and political activity. Political activity is a calling, a mandate, and an activity which may honor the Creator. Hence, we do not begin by viewing government as inherently evil or malicious. It is not merely a "necessary evil." Ruling or dominion is an activity assigned to humans before the Fall, not as a necessary evil resulting from the entrance of sin into the world. Although no specific form

---

14:40), this study follows the sequence of revelation, observing a sense of progress.

of government is indicated at this early stage, the first week of creation does validate orderly government as a divine commission.

The Priority of Family: Mini-commonwealths

The first sphere of government in the Bible is the human family. From the earliest of times in the OT, God charged the family with certain responsibilities—the family preceding the civil government by hundreds of years. Actually the state is not even a creation ordinance nor even formally regulated until about 1400 BC at Sinai. Sensitive to that established priority, one will seek to structure society accordingly. Throughout, it is maintained that the family's responsibilities should not be usurped by the state.

It is God, not the state, who ordains families. The family is God's idea—not the possession of the latest sociologists, the state, nor even the church. The family is not an accident, nor the result of social compact theory. Some skeptics would admit that the family is antiquated but contend that paleo-lithic grandparents (sic) just happened to merge into families. Others argue that the family evolved together out of the necessity to protect one another. To these, the family is not ordained by God; it is only an accident of human survival. Under that view, neither the state nor families will follow God's design.

However, the family is much more than that; it is a covenant unit. God is the Designer of families according to Scripture. God, the Creator of families, did not design the family to be a mere social convenience, but to be a vessel appointed and prepared by him to carry out his work. The family is a created ministry unit with specific duties, structures, and responsibilities.

Consider the early chapters of Genesis, recalling that it is important *where* a subject is first addressed in God's Word. When Adam and Eve sinned, a drastic and prevailing tendency was introduced to the world. In Genesis 3, after sin entered the world, everything was altered. Prior to the Fall, the first two chapters of the Bible depict a world none of us have ever known—a universe in which sin did not have its thraldom.

Those early chapters of Genesis afford a clearer view of what God intends by his creation. The family is still intact after the Fall, but to see its original purpose, consider what is taught about the family prior to the Fall.

The family is *the original society from which the state and church (and every other organization) emerge.*[15] That amazingly simple idea, unfortunately, is sometimes forgotten or its impact on the state is minimized. Parents and the family are primarily to nurture the young. Parents cannot delegate to others the sole care for the children the Lord has given them. We live in an age in which individuals—even fine Christian individuals—lust to transfer God-given responsibilities to others. Sometimes, Christians even seek to delegate to the church or the state that which only the home can do. Neither the church nor the state is called to raise and nurture in place of the family. Even the best of churches or states can never substitute or replace parents.

The responsible parent will also be very careful not to hand children over to the state or to any other religious entity. If parents are not careful, they will allow the state to educate their children in sexual morals, to attack religion, or to train them to look for other than scriptural solutions. Parents are ordained by God and are accountable to him to guard the briefly entrusted treasure. That the family is the model for the state (and not vice-versa) is seen by Isaiah's comparison of rulers to gentle fathers (Is. 49:23).

Even in the greatest of educational systems, parents are not commanded to hand their children over as wards of the state, even if the system will provide many services. Instead of discharging the valuable nurture of children to others, Christians should recall: The family is the normal school in which training in righteousness is first taught. Those young years, with children in the "Nursery of the

---

[15] John Frame, "Toward a Theology of the State," sees the state as a function of the extended family: "What we see in Scripture, rather, is a kind of gradual development from family authority to something which we would tend to call a state. The borderline between family and state is not sharp or clear." Cf. *Westminster Theological Journal*, vol. 51, no. 2 (Fall 1989), 206.

church," provide numerous opportunities to teach the things of God to children while they are like wet cement.

Post World War II German theologian Helmut Thielicke offers a finely nuanced perspective in speaking of the state as "a secondary order as compared with the paternal office. It is secondary because its authority is derived from that of the paternal office and because, unlike the latter, it is an emergency order and not an order of creation."[16]

Many other structures, methods, and beliefs will come and go, but God will continue to use the family. It is his idea. G. K. Chesterton asserted: "The family is radically subversive of the state-control." What he meant was that the family was the one institution that the state could not possess, enslave, intimidate, nor control. He said, "If we wish to preserve the family we must revolutionize the nation."[17]

As Genesis unfolds, *Adam was given a family that actually constituted a commonwealth in miniature.* The earliest sphere of government was the family; it was a small state. "The family is the model state," said Benjamin M. Palmer.[18] Long before mammoth governmental bureaucracies, and long before the growth of democracies, society was ordered in simple fashion—in families. These performed basic tasks in lieu of civil government performing them: they cared for one another, they protected from enemies, and they passed on values and wealth. The family is a sufficient government. In fact, if government crumbled or if a cataclysmic holocaust occurred, the survivors would probably begin with the new state based on the family.

---

[16] Helmut Thielicke, *Theological Ethics: Politics* (Grand Rapids: Eerdmans, 1979), 287. He continues: "Whether in fact such a minimum can be attained depends on whether there is a mature and legitimate counterpart that can stand over against the state, or whether in the field of education, e.g., the state is the only power involved or is faced with a mature and authentic competitor in the church, particularly the community of believing parents."

[17] G. K. Chesterton, *Brave New Family* (San Francisco: Ignatius, 1990), 24.

[18] Benjamin Palmer, *The Family in its Civil and Churchly Aspects* (1876, rpr. Greenville, SC: Greenville Presbyterian Theological Seminary Press, 1992), 174.

After the Fall, Adam and Eve had other children. Organized as a family, they worked together, herded flocks together, passed on religious lessons together; they sinned, too. By Cain and Abel's time, the very presence of a tithing and sacrificial system points to the fact that Adam and Eve were teaching their children valuable and religious lessons.

After Cain killed Abel, one of the aspects of punishment was that he was excluded from his family. He was sentenced to be a non-family member, a restless wanderer on the earth (4:12). Cain realized what exclusion from the family signified and lamented that this sentence was too great for him to bear. It was a paramount loss to be excluded from the family. Cain moved on from place to place in search of family. Finally, Cain had children (4:17) and built a city. The family government and structure was present there, as well.

Genesis 5 presents a genealogy that traces the people, not by wealth nor talent, but by family origin. When God sent the flood in Genesis 6, it was not Noah alone who was saved in the ark, but his family. At the flood, eight people entered the boat. God saved this covenant family as a family unit.

Until the time of Abraham, the next genealogies are in terms of families. In Genesis 12, God appeared to Abraham and ordered him to leave and follow him. So Abraham, childless at that time, took his wife and his nephew, Lot, to the land of Canaan (12:5). Along the way God spoke to Abraham and promised to give that land of Canaan to the family of Abraham, to his offspring (12:7; cf. also Gen. 15:5). Genesis portrays human history in familial rather than individualistic terms.

Since these early times, faith and the family have been the dynamics God uses.[19] By the time of the New Testament all believers are portrayed as being in this family of Abraham. All who believe like Abraham did (Gal. 3:12-18) are incorporated into his family. Throughout the Book of Genesis, Abraham teaches young

---

[19] Cf. George Grant's "Three Essential Elements of Biblical Charity: Faith, Family, and Work," *Welfare Reformed: A Compassionate Approach* (Franklin, TN: Legacy, 1994), 68-83 which also stresses these themes.

Isaac. Isaac then selects a wife for Jacob. God's very name in Genesis is associated with a family succession: the God of Abraham, Isaac, and Jacob. God has not forsaken the family. The family is, "the ultimate human institution . . . Christianity, even enormous as was its revolution, did not alter this ancient and savage sanctity; it merely reversed it."[20]

That this familial basis of civil order endured may be noted from the fact that much of the Book of Proverbs is concerned with the family and its instruction of children. From its outset Solomon writes, "Listen my son to your father's instruction and do not forsake your mother's teaching" (1:8). Parents are the first teachers of the family, and children are instructed by God to heed their teaching if they would be wise. Proverbs 2:1 says, "My son, if you accept my words and store up my commands . . . you will understand the fear of the Lord." Proverbs 3:1 says: "My son, do not forget my teaching, but keep my commands in your heart, for they will prolong your life . . ." (Cf. also Prov. 4:1.) Nearly all of the early chapters of Proverbs present this picture: children are in the school of the parents who instruct in the paths of wisdom. Nations have learned the hard way throughout history what happens if that order is not preserved. Chesterton is again perceptive: "This is the social structure of mankind, far older than all its records and more universal than any of its religions; and all attempts to alter it are mere talk and tomfoolery."[21] He asserted, "When we defend the family we do not mean it is always a peaceful family; when we maintain the thesis of marriage we do not mean that it is always a happy marriage. We mean that it is the theater of the spiritual drama, the place where things happen, especially the things that matter."[22]

Frequently, people assume that the key to societal success is in passing certain legislative remedies. Yet, that approach overlooks that often the most important and most enduring things in life are non-political. The family, as God's creation, is a non-political

---

[20] Chesterton, *Brave New Family*, 37.

[21] Chesterton, op. cit., 57.

[22] Chesterton, op. cit., 24.

component. Yet, it has enormous political ramification. The family is the foundation block for government; not vice-versa.

As a creation ordinance, God established and sanctified the family. Normal livelihood came as a man would leave his father and mother (Gen. 2:22-23) and set up his own home. A certain industriousness and labor-orientation is assumed by this. Good political solutions will seek to honor this order and not legislate specific policy activities that contradict this basis. In short, if a particular political plan is found to stultify the family-order, then *it* must be changed, not the family order.

To the earthly politician nothing could seem more absurd than to emphasize something as simple as building up families or calling on homes to worship in order to renew the state. Yet that may be one of the grandest things Christians can do for their culture. Whatever makes good citizens makes a country better; family worship makes better citizens. Regular worship builds in the notions of fixed-law, obedience, duty, and authority. Christians pray for their government, pay taxes, and strengthen communities. Nations may even be affected by prayers (Rev. 8:1-4). In the nineteenth century, James W. Alexander noted, "Christianity compacts the structure, and strengthens every wall. It adds a new cement, and makes the father more a father—the husband more a husband—the son more a son; so that there is not a social tie which does not become more strong and endearing by means of grace."

Christian citizenship is best passed on by the family. Unfortunately, many parents have not always passed on this important baton. The recent demise of politics and the resulting all-time-low approval ratings for politicians, to some degree, belongs at the doorstep of Christians. Christians have not always transmitted the vital political lessons to their children.

Rather than taking a hands-off posture, afraid that they might impose their values on children, in matters of citizenship Christians should teach their children while they are young. In terms of civic responsibilities, Proverbs 22:6 applies as well: "Train up a child in the way that he should go and when he is old he will not depart from it." Numerous studies have confirmed the influence of the home in shaping political loyalty and voting patterns. Routinely, voters say that their parents' political affiliation had a major impact on their underlying political views. Christians can no longer afford to see politics as a matter to be left only to the experts.

Some time ago, our church hosted a conference in which we brought in several leading experts on the interface between Christianity and politics. One of the speakers was based in a Washington think-tank and had earlier served as a Special Assistant to President Reagan. As far as policy matters, he is one of the leaders in the world and a devoted Christian.

At the time, a large segment of Christians were distraught over the election. Amidst that frenzy, this quiet-spirited man advocated one of the most insightful but lasting things. It was quite simple. In response to what Christians could do for the upcoming election, and how they could exert influence, he threw the audience a curve. Doug Bandow, former assistant to President Reagan, did *not* tell this group to sign up as activists (although that has its place), nor to write cards to congressmen; nor did he advocate attendance at political rallies. His curve ball was to remind Christians how much they could teach about politics in the home. Christians could best influence the world in that fashion. That simple arena—the home—is a given, and parents who have sound views on political matters can teach those to their children as a part of basic Christian discipleship. Parents can take these opportunities to train their children to see even political matters through the lens of Scripture and to apply biblical truth to such matters. A generation of consistent discipleship in this area would produce a seismic shift in public policy.

Parental discipleship in political ideas is a common and ordinary matter, yet it holds much promise to improve the state. Stronger, more discipled families holds much more promise than the panting leftism of the 1960s. Children should be discipled in the home in every area possible. For the Christian family, there is no matter ("not an inch of the universe," as Abraham Kuyper said) that is not under the scrutiny of the Lord Christ. As Christians structure life's matters, they do so first in allegiance to biblical principles. The family structure is repeated in Genesis 7:7, 9:9, and 12:1. Families are essential to proper government. Families may operate with and apart from the state in some cases, but in no cases can the state operate without the family.

Over a century ago, it was observed: "The early constitution of society was formed before the state had any existence. To the family the state is indebted for its origin, and civil society reaches its highest end as a more extended family bound together by domestic ties."[23] William A. Cocke argued that, "An immense error has been imbibed from our early studies of Grecian and Roman philosophy, as well as from their jurisprudence, in supposing that the state or common-wealth existed before the family government; and that the state received from civil society its constitution. This vast error has corrupted the tone of modern . . . political philosophy, as to the priority of the origin of the two societies, domestic and civil; for historically and logically the former is not only older, but the true source and fountain-head of the latter."[24] He concluded: "From the necessity of protection to the family sprang the state, and the power of civil society. . . . the civil power is the immediate offspring of the family power; and this is the explanation of the text, 'For there is no power but of God.'"[25]

Politics Disrupted and Human Depravity: The Fall

The second and third chapters of Genesis present God the Creator in the role of king or law-maker. In Genesis 2:17, God established the terms, rules, and benefits for this early garden-nation. He gave positive instructions to Adam as well as clear prohibitions. Later, after the Fall (Gen. 3:13-18), God meted out enduring sentences for those who had broken his law. Thus early on, law had a place in this rule, and creatures were responsible to the law-giver. A true and blessed theocracy existed and was sufficient.

---

[23] William Archer Cocke, "The Religious Principle The Life of the Nation," *The Southern Presbyterian Review*, Vol. XXII (July, 1871), 352.
[24] Idem.
[25] Ibid., 353.

Biblically, a major change-point occurred in Genesis 3. With this Fall comes the beginning of human conflict and the need for restraining government. In fact, the cursings by God (Gen. 3:16-19) materially altered the environment, resulting in interpersonal enmity, difficult labor, strife, and a host of other dynamics that both underlie the need for the state and also find their ultimate remedy only in the Creator. Nonetheless, as solutions are sought it may be helpful to observe how and when this problem originated. In addition, with a fallen universe as a constant in policy formulations, resulting political efforts will be delimited from seeking either utopian or totalitarian means and ends. A proper appreciation of the Fall supports Ronald Nash's comment: "No economic or political system that assumes the essential goodness of human nature or holds out the dream of a perfect earthly society can possibly be consistent with the Biblical world view."[26] Realism about depravity must be included in any effective formulation of human politics. It is a *sine qua non.* Failure to factor in the persistent dynamic of human depravity commits the state not only to political naivete but also to governmental inadequacy or danger.

Depravity may be defined as "how sin affects every aspect, or the totality, of human personality." Not only does sin affect our morality but also the very way we think and act. It colors the range of human activity and taints our world. Prior to Adam, this did not exist.

I grew up in the southern United States during the post WWII baby boom. Somehow, the main churches talking about sin when I grew up were those that defined sin in a very Victorian and limited manner; it was primarily a moral or sexual sin. I know they did not mean to convey that, but that is what I got out of it. Or maybe it was because I was a teenager and those were about all that some folks thought about.

However, the more I studied Scripture and the more honest I was with myself, the clearer it became to me—as one theologian said, "The only purely empirical doctrine is the doctrine of sin." Painfully, I came to understand that depravity ran so deep that it

---

[26] Ronald Nash, *Poverty and Wealth* (Westchester, IL: Crossway, 1986), 62.

was not superficial at all; it could not be scraped off. It was at the heart of our problems because it was in our hearts.

Total depravity is seen today in:

1. How we will shop for a counselor to agree with an unbiblical moral act.
2. How we automatically assume that when something happens the other fellow is wrong or up to no good.
3. How quick we are to devise governmental bailouts.

Three years ago, there was much pressure in the USA to have the government bailout several large mortgage lenders and other businesses. On the surface, the argument was made that to fail to do so will spawn even more economic problems. Thus, the assumptions that support that policy are that: (1) the central government's charter includes bailing out private entities, whose collapse might lead to further economic deterioration; (2) all slumps are catastrophic; (3) users who have over borrowed, or lenders who have over extended, must not bear all consequences; and (4) further taxation to fund such bailouts may be assumed by the government without prior approval.

Certainly, folks with interest in this issue may claim an unparalleled state of events to justify government intervention, but reasoned analysts might also measure the magnitude of any perceived crisis differently if a longer stretch of history had been considered as a basis of comparison. This kind of interventionism shares "the mistaken belief that governmental intervention in economic matters can successfully achieve desired results while still falling short of the total controls that characterize a socialist system."[27] Economic programs, thus, are not as value-free as some imagine, and frequently many modern proposals are more reminiscent of Marx's manifesto than of proposals that are based on sounder economic theory like allowing the free market to correct itself by eliminating those who unjustly over extended

---

[27] James Gills and Ronald Nash, *A Biblical Economics Manifesto* (Lake Mary, Florida: Creation House, 2002), 31.

themselves which makes opportunity for new businesses to efficiently operate. Many of these ideas on bailouts fit more with human perfectionism than thorough depravity.

4. How you jockey for position or prominence.
5. In the Church . . .
    a. A person will leave if he doesn't get his way on some small issue; and some Christians are smart enough to make all issues "ultimate."
    b. If a person cannot serve as a leader . . . he'll hike right off. That is often more an expression of depravity than it is courage.
    c. We seek to have benefits go to our family or group.
6. In Welfare, why you need accountability.
7. In liberal arts studies, why history omits certain things. Often, for example, the role of faith is barely, if ever, included in certain histories.
8. Other people's children that hang out; oh wait, did your own escape the curse of the Fall? Do you trust them?

God knew, and John Calvin courageously preached, that believers will be better prepared to function and serve God if they *understand something of the environment of depravity that surrounds us.* The knowledge of Total Depravity, thus, *forms our set of expectations.* Scripture clearly teaches this **realistic** idea; that may be one of the large differences, too: realism or unrealism.

Calvinists and others should assess the nature of man before advocating remedies for any problems or scarcities. While Calvin's biblical faith was clear that the universe, including man, had changed dramatically and substantially from how it had begun. Calvin noted that prior to the Fall, the world was "a most fair and delightful mirror of the divine favor," whereas afterwards it and human beings were "cursed."[28] The post-Fall world, along with all

---

[28] John Calvin, *Commentaries on the First Book of Moses* (1554, rpr. Grand Rapids: Baker Book House, 1979), 173. References to this commentary in parentheses in this section are taken from this edition.

its culture was characterized by a "dreadful alienation" (173) and servile conditions. This fallen world was the antithesis of the "pleasant labor in which Adam previously employed himself, that in a sense he might be said to play; for he was not formed for idleness but for action." (174) In the cursed conditions, however, the "sweet delight" of cultivation was exchanged for "servile work . . . as if he were condemned to the mines."[29] (174) Once sin entered the world, it would be impossible, following Adam's sin, for one to plan on man being good, fair, righteous, or benevolent all on his own. To the contrary, because of the Fall man's depravity must be factored into every human endeavor, including politics and policy. The resulting thorns that pained Adam would make work hazardous and less enjoyable.

Commenting on the effect of the Fall, Calvin explained that the hunger of men and animals "must be attributed to the corruption of nature." Nature went from the "fair order" which once subsisted "by God's original appointment" to barrenness, crop failure, inclemency, drought, hail, and "whatever is disorderly in the world, [which] are the fruits of sin."[30] In contrast to the perfect economy before the Fall, our inherited economic culture is characterized by corruption, travail, oppression, vengeance, and divine wrath. The once-harmonious economic order now suffers major inequities and disruptions.

Calvin spoke of the human heart as "insidious," "vicious," and "accursed." (vol. 9, 353) The prophet Jeremiah had to bring this warning because of the callousness of the Jews, who were "wanton and obstinate." And Calvin knew that the problem was the human heart, not merely the external actions. *Depravity carried its own inscrutibility.* God, the searcher of all hearts, wanted Israel to know that they could not fool him. He saw their wickedness and "fallaciousness" (355) plainly. All human cunning is in vain, even

---

[29] It is in this context that Calvin also views work as far more than manual labor. He condemns those who would "rashly impel all men to manual labor," and believed there was a legitimate place for "mechanical arts" and many forms of work. (175)

[30] Calvin on Gen. 3:19; cited in Andre Bieler, *Calvin's Economic and Social Thought* (Geneva: World Alliance of Reformed Churches, 2005), 211.

if folks attempt to hide "their thoughts as it were under the earth, that is, while they thought that by their false pretences they could deceive God as well as men." (355)

With "specious pretext" and "guile," men cannot deceive God. Such overconfidence "inebriates" human minds. **Even if we fool ourselves, we do not fool God.**

Due to the Fall, a Golden Age in which all humans glorify God with their wealth is not anticipated prior to the New Jerusalem. This should be acknowledged in policy formulations; instead a rose-colored view, we expect selfishness, conflict, theft, destruction of property, and strife in economic and business sectors. Rather than live in denial of such fallen realities, enduring solutions that factor in such selfishness will be more reliable. If one begins, however, expecting a utopia, he will quickly become frustrated with the amount of fallenness in our universe. Additionally, realism in business and profit sectors is a better beginning point than utopianism. Thus, Calvinism explains what and why to expect in the marketplace as it understands the nature of man. The children of Calvin will be profoundly and inevitably dystopian.

A definite anthropology (or view of man's nature) flows from Calvin's teaching. In a sermon from the book of Galatians, Calvin said, *"If we were all like angels, blameless and freely able to exercise perfect self-control, we would not need rules or regulations.* Why, then, do we have so many laws and statutes? Because of man's wickedness, for he is constantly overflowing with evil; this is why a remedy is required."[31] James Madison would write two centuries later in the Federalist, almost as if copying Calvin, observing that the innate tendency toward sinfulness and the exploitation of others required that governmental power be circumscribed. To Madison, it was but "a reflection on human nature, that such devices should be necessary to control the abuses of government." Madison reflected the thought of John Knox—who was mentored in the Calvinistic

---

[31] John Calvin, *Sermons on Galatians* (Edinburgh: Banner of Truth Trust, 1996), 313. Emphasis added.

politics of Geneva, only to transport such ideas back to his native Scotland, and ultimately to America—when he wrote: "But what is government itself, but the greatest of all reflections on human nature? *If men were angels, no government would be necessary.* If angels were to govern men, neither external nor internal controls on government would be necessary" (*Federalist* #51). Had Madison derived his view from human experience alone, this reference would merit little comment. However, it appears remarkably similar to a particular theological formulation from several centuries earlier and derived from a common well.

If, as Calvin said, men were sinless, no fiscal accountability or external structures would be necessary. Each person would work hard, produce more, steward with excellence, and benevolently share. However, the principle of selfishness would call for the following truths to be anticipated as effects of the Fall on politics.

You might be a Depravitarian if . . .

Taking off on Jeff Foxworthy's "You might be a Redneck if . . ." routine, "You might be a Depravitarian if . . .":

a. … you understand that folks will try to steal in markets and be greedy; and perhaps be on your guard against it. Watch for scams; if it's too good to be true …

b. . . . you believe we need laws and that criminals will exist until heaven.

c. … Inspect expenditures—a deacon once advised me too late: "It's always someone close to you who will steal; yet we trust folks time and time again."

d. … Ministers need to be examined before assuming pulpits.

e. . . . All speakers have an agenda or bias (that is postmodernism's one nugget of truth) . . .

f. . . . you believe that your own children have a sin nature and that no matter where they grow up, how they're educated, or even how committed their parents are, they will sin.

g. . . . you expect little from Big Brother and more from yourself as a father/mother.
h. . . . you are skeptical of claims that all scientists are automatically objective and never had agendas.
i. The blindness of evil which takes human beings, made in the image of God, and automatically defines some as subhuman because of their color, race, handicap.

Depravity has much value for business theory and practice. To fail to anticipate it is to beg for multiple mistakes based on seriously flawed assumptions. Put another way, *realism about one's neighbor will call for the expectation that sin, crime, harm, oppression, evil, aggression, and war will occur.* Businesses and individuals are prudent to plan on those. Calvin's picture of the fully fallen man requires nothing short of a productive work ethic supported by accountability. This accountability needs to be undergirded by a strong legal system and the free movement of wages, labor, opportunities and consequences. A Calvinistic grasp of man's depravity leaves the concept of collectivism found wanting; man's sinfulness is incongruent with the socialistic requirement of self-sacrifice and altruism. Economic systems are advanced by the providence of God, who uses wealth, the work ethic, and the open market as a few of the visible means to advance his will upon this earth.

The believer who knows God's Word on this subject, instead of thinking that all things will turn out rosy, will:

- Expect sin
- Calculate sin
- Know that it will affect you, not only others outside your home. We have a tendency to be very adroit at finding all the sin in others' lives but in our own …
- Politicians are sinful; why preachers are.
- We think sinfully: that is what the "noetic affect of sin" is; our very understanding is tainted.
- Sin lives in this church, in the regional church, and in the national assembly.

My wife is a big Charles H. Spurgeon fan. I often hear her counseling a person to employ Spurgeon's three steps to watch sin:

Expect
Detect
Reject

Our will is bound in sin. We cannot choose God, apart from the working of his Holy Spirit. That affects the way you do evangelism, what you expect, and how you lead your church. It certainly affects politics. And believers in Scripture must remain vigilant not to vastly overestimate the human will and ability.

Helmut Thielicke argues that, "apart from knowledge of the Fall there is nothing but myth, in this case the mythologizing of powers and processes. By 'mythologizing' we mean that 'things' are taken to be divine or demonic powers; they are endowed with souls and made into living creatures. Theologically viewed, myth is a process of repression and an act of evasion: man regards himself as innocent, held in the hands of seducing powers, because it is in his interest to conceal or look away from his own hand and culpability."[32] He also maintains: "From a theological standpoint one might say that the distribution of powers is an institutional expression of an abiding mistrust of power, or rather of the people in power. The call for a distribution of powers is a partly conscious and partly unconscious recognition of the reality of the Fall and the unreliability of fallen man."[33] Citing Montesquieu's division of power into legislative power, executive power, and judicial power (as early as 1748) as a corollary of human depravity, Thielicke warns against the state possessing "uncontrolled, monopolized power. By guarding against the misuse of power, the distribution of powers thus has the positive task of safeguarding freedom, of making freedom possible in the political sphere where a variety of power constructs necessarily arise."[34] He argues that, "Democracy

---

[32] Helmut Thielicke, *Theological Ethics: Politics* (Grand Rapids: Eerdmans, 1979), 176.
[33] Ibid., 210.

provides for a distribution of powers precisely because it knows the danger of power."[35]

The fact of sin in society dictates that solutions cannot be obtained through utopian schemes. The OT manifests a realism, a startling absence of utopianism, not expecting that all societal ills will be eradicated by some program, political movement, or institution. The fact of sin insures the need for the state. The state is necessitated by human depravity and the Fall and, as such, is a mechanism of response to that fallen condition. Both civil and ecclesiastical forms of government are necessitated by the Fall and depravity.

Of course, even in a perfect world, government would be needed for order, rank, and efficiency. For example, even the angelic beings appear to be ranked in orders with "rulers, authorities, powers, and dominions" (Eph. 1:21). Divine government is present within the Trinity before the foundation of the world (Jn. 17:21-24) and will also be evident in heaven (cf. Rev. 4-5). Hence, government is not an exclusively negative or restraining concept. It has a proper place. However, between the Fall and the Last Day *(eschaton)*, the state will always have a restraining element.

Government as given by God is purposefully erected to restrain the unjust and protect the just. If humans in some state of nature were able to act "upon their honor," as it were, then government would not be needed. As Madison said of human government, "If men were angels no government would be necessary." If Marxism could have demonstrated altruism, or if uninterrupted progress could produce a species free of depravity, then indeed civil government might not be so important. Even optimistic orthodox views of sanctification do not lead us to expect a perfectionism that will eventually eradicate the need for government and structure. If one expects people to be sinners, then the best form of government will strive to limit—although not eradicate—such ill-effects of sin.[36]

---

[34] Ibid., 215-216.

[35] Ibid., 216.

[36] For a fuller discussion of this theme, particularly with application to church government, see *Paradigms in Polity*, David W. Hall and Joseph H. Hall, eds.

Therefore, governments have been constructed with checks and balances, the best of which provide for regular and thoughtful means of accountability. Most Christians acknowledge that to achieve this, constitutions must follow the faithful patterns of God. Such constitutions serve to delimit unbridled subjectivity and will-reign, exhibiting a firm belief in the need to limit the power of any individual. Abraham Kuyper surmised:

> Calvin's profound conception of sin is likewise the outcome of the recognition of the sovereignty of God. . . . he was republican because he knows that even kings are sinners, who yield to temptation perhaps more readily than their subjects, inasmuch as their temptations are greater. . . . He knows equally well that the self-same sin moves the masses, and that, hence resistance, insurrection, and mutinies will not end, unless a righteous constitution bridles the abuse of authority, marks off its boundaries, and offers the people a natural protection against despotism and ambitious schemes.[37]

Hence, constitutionalism fosters a restraint on sin. It is sin, however, that demands a subsequent form of government. Our theology of sin and our anthropology are the values that shape our consequent civil government. Theology thus molds polity.

If the above is admitted, then it is a constant value to seek to appropriate biblical government. Furthermore, the Bible's information and instructions on matters of civil government are equally matters of revelation, as are its statements pertaining to salvation, social responsibility, prayer, or providence. Hence, the sincere disciple will want to know God's mind on this matter (2 Tim. 3:16). James H. Thornwell helpfully pointed out:

> While we admit that questions of government are subordinate in importance to questions of faith—mere trifles compared with the great truths of the Gospel . . . it does not follow that they are of *no*

(Grand Rapids: Eerdmans, 1994), chapter 2.

[37] Abraham Kuyper, "Calvinism: The Origin and Safeguard of Our Constitutional Liberties," *Bibliotheca Sacra*, October, 1895, 665-666.

> value. . . . Because . . . government is not the great thing, it does not follow that it is nothing. . . . We wish to study the *whole* will of God, and we wish to give everything precisely that prominence which He designs that it should occupy in His own Divine economy.[38]

To the extent that one is committed to know that "whole counsel of God" (Acts 20:28), civil government will be a part of the Christian mind. Thorough commitment to be submissive to the whole counsel of God, even in the spheres of government, is one of the distinguishing marks of biblical Christianity. The Christian will cling to all that God has revealed about government or any other subject, as long as the revelation is properly interpreted. Believers will stubbornly refuse to act as editors or evaluators who seek to prioritize canons within canons of Holy Writ. *All* scripture is inspired and profitable—even the verses that inform about civil structure or government. Evidently, God did not think these subjects were beneath the dignity of revelation. Hence, one wishes to benefit from the Bible's revealed organizational corpus, as well as from its revealed soteriological corpus. Both have the same divine origin.

The fact of sin should have a permanent and profound impact on any formulation of the role of the state. The Bible further corroborates that sin is transcultural (cf. Gen. 6:5, 8:21) and resident in the innermost motivations of the human heart. No human government will be pleasing to God if it does not calculate the significance of human depravity. Thus, wise political decisions will remain cognizant of this.

A Genesis Miscellany of Biblical Wisdom

As one begins to question politics, he will also note that the early chapters of Genesis demonstrate that God governs the eco-system.

---

[38] *The Collected Works of James Henley Thornwell,* Vol. IV, 294 (Edinburgh: Banner of Truth, 1986).

According to Genesis 6:7, God is free to destroy certain aspects of the eco-system. While it should not be underestimated that humans are appointed to be "stewards" of God's creation, their role is a delegated one and should not be confused with the role of "owner." God alone is the owner of the eco-system (Ps. 24:1), and he is ultimately responsible for it. The state may regulate certain aspects of human behavior regarding it, but must not philosophically confuse itself with divinity in its attempt to preserve the environment. With the many environmental movements of late, these two facts above, i.e., (1) the fact of depravity and imperfection, and (2) the responsibility of God as Creator and Owner of the eco-system, must temper political plans to preserve the ecosphere.

Capital punishment is also one of the earliest matters introduced that is normally assigned to the state. In these earliest cases, however, the governments were familial or tribal. Many assume a "state" to enforce capital sentences, and thus infer that the origin of human government was shortly after the time of Noah.

Although some have viewed Genesis 9:6 as authorizing the family to execute capital punishment,[39] the majority of Christian theologians have recognized the state as the proper agency to perform capital punishment. Robert Culver has argued that Augustine, Luther, Calvin and other leading theologians located the origin of the state *qua* institution in the regulation of capital punishment.

> Protestant identification of this text with the original formal establishment of coercive human government begins with Martin Luther. Luther's views of the divine origin and authority of civil government were prevalent in seventeenth and eighteenth century Britain and British America. . . . Having pointed out that Cain was punished only by excommunication, Luther adds: 'Here, however, God shares his power with man and grants him power over life and death among men, provided that the person is guilty of shedding blood . . .' Luther finds the establishment of all coercive government forces here: 'here God establishes government and

---

[39] John Frame, op. cit., 206.

gives it the sword, to hold wantonness in check, lest violence and other sins proceed without limit.'[40]

Culver draws eight propositions from Genesis 9:6, summarized below.

1. First, civil government is for "the protection, conservation, fostering, and improvement of human life. . . . Government has a general design for weal here at inception."

2. Second, government does not have its origin in some primeval social contract among our ancestors, as Hobbes, Locke, Rousseau, and their secular democratic followers would have it; neither does it arise out of some immanent force in the world culminating in the state, as supposed Hegel and certain other later nineteenth century German philosophers. It has its origin specifically in God's decree. He alone is sovereign, but has delegated the power of civil government to magistrates—the manner of their placement not being specified.

3. Third, the humane civil organization of men must have a moral basis. This has its negative requirement in forbidding killing of man for reasons of personal revenge. It has its positive side in making each man owe a debt of love to his neighbor (Rom. 13:8-9).

4. This is closely connected, in the fourth place, with the religious foundation of civil government, "for in the image of God made he man" (Gen. 9:6). This is a fact of divine

---

[40] Robert D. Culver, "Civil Government with Coercive Power: Of Special Divine Origin or Simply A Development in History?" unpublished paper delivered to the Evangelical Theological Society, November 1993. Culver summarizes: "Except for the commentators who, rejecting the presence of authentic history in the passage, make it a sort of anachronism from Israel's monarchial times, almost every grammatical commentary and theological treatment gives this obvious and undoubted interpretation—C. F. Keil, F. Delitzsch and J. G. Murphy, are examples among older exegetical writers; H. C. Leupold among more recent. Erich Sauer, a contemporary European writer; and A. J. McClain and John Murray, recent American writers on biblical theology, have expressed similar views. In a class by himself is C. S. Lewis, whose powerful pen also struck some mighty blows on this subject."

revelation and is not only a matter of religious faith but of veritable reality.

5. "The institution of government with coercive power shows that fallen humanity . . . has unmeasured potentialities for evil which must be curbed. That the biblical sentence quoted describes formal, collective action by man is indicated by the Hebrew idiom, which employs the generic term for mankind rather than the individual person, and by the fact that it is followed immediately by 'for in the image of God made he him.' This would be meaningless if the sentence in question were a simple prediction that murderers will be killed somehow by other people. It is quite usual in the Hebrew language for commands of God or of kings, governors, or presumably of parents, to be expressed by the simple future indicative form while conveying the imperative mood."

6. The death penalty for murder, the ultimate crime against one's neighbor, is not merely personal revenge by the dead man's family against his murderer, but divine vengeance, the just retribution upon the offender for wrong done against the God in whose image every man has been made.

7. We have here the primary *raison d'etre* for all penalty or punishment—not *reformation* of the culprit primarily (which in the case of murderers is certainly out of the question if they are executed), not *protection* of society (though society is protected), and not *prevention* of further crimes, though that is desirable—but the purpose of God to *vindicate* himself as governor of the universe. For this reason, Christian writers commonly speak of divine punishments—in this case delegated in execution to magistrates—as vindicative (but not vindictive).[41]

---

[41] John Ponet also argued that this ordinance exemplified how laws should be made without exempting the legislators. Rather legislators were to "set apart all affections, and to observe an equality in meting out pains, that they be not greater or less, than the fault deserves, and that they not punish the innocent . . ." John Ponet, *A Short Treatise on Political Power* (forthcoming: *Reformation Political Tracts*, Patrick Poole, ed.).

8. Eighth and finally, the moral justification for the institution of human government and for the capital punishment of murder is the sacredness of human life—man's dignity as a responsible being: "Another way of saying this is that it is man's relatedness to God, as created in the image of God, that demands that he receive treatment as a morally responsible being rather than a thing or commodity, the irresponsible creature of heredity and environment. Take a murderer promptly to court, convict and punish him just as promptly, and you treat him as a responsible man. Treat him as a mere victim of his environment and history, attempt merely to rehabilitate him from his murdering tendencies, and you treat him as a thing or commodity to be manipulated."[42]

Such study is the fruit of posing a hard, political question and seeking a sound biblical answer. There are many other such areas where this yields reliable guidance.

Nation Building?

The tower of Babel is one of the earliest biblical instances of multi-national confederations. It was hoped that this linguistic homogeneity would provide a human means of state-preservation. Yet, it is apparent that God does not condone this multi-national approach, a warning against an ecumenical foreign policy. Indeed, many of the problems that modern states face have been brought about by imperialism (the attempt to conquer and gain nations) and entanglements resulting from over-extensive treaties. Over-extensive foreign aid and treaties may haunt the state.

While it is clear that God creates and permits various states of diverse sizes, there is no command to assimilate all nations into a single human state. The only state that will be successful in doing

---

[42] Culver, op. cit., also believes that John Locke saw the divine origination of a coercive civil power in the era of the flood. John Ponet, in *A Short Treatise on the Political Power* (1556), also agreed that there was no capital punishment until after the Flood.

that is the Monarchy of the Messiah. Invariably, when nations seek to expand and assimilate inimical notions into their culture or their worship, their government suffers. While we are not prepared to say that the Bible teaches strict isolationism, on the other hand, expansion-ism—whether by forceful imperialism or by moral treaties—and its attendant responsibilities has led to numerous instances of unnecessary war, high taxes, poor policy, and the loss of life.

For example, Woodrow Wilson's desire for a League of Nations was the beginning of a host of other entanglements (the United Nations, agreements to support NATO members, Southeast Asian involvements, etc.) in the twentieth century that drained billions of tax dollars from a country that should have also attended to its own problems and needs. The Tower of Babel serves to warn modern states that there is no mandate to gather together all nations into one form of government. Indeed such centralization is condemned by this passage (Gen. 11:6-9). In that case, God seems to favor decentralization and effected it by his providence.

This episode may also be an example of an early humanistic state. If so, then one can see that later humanistic states are not new, and their dynamics are likely unchanged either. Any state that enshrines a false religion, thereby attempting to divinize itself and its agencies, is eschewed by this revelation. God—not the citizens—must be the center of the state. Genesis 14 evidences the early employment of confederacies for battle. Kederlaomer reigned over a confederacy with four other kings (Gen. 14:2-4) for a twelve-year period before a revolution. Other primitive states were allied into military confederacies as well (Gen. 14:6-11; 26:28). At about 2000 BC, Kederlaomer raided Sodom and captured Abraham's nephew, Lot (Gen. 14:12). Abraham then called upon his own trained militia (Gen. 14:14) and pursued the strongest king in the region, Kederlaomer. Abraham and his confederacy (Gen. 14:13) defeated the Kederlaomer alliance and met with other kings after the victory (Gen. 14:17).

One such king was Melchizedek, the king of Salem (Gen. 14:18). The notion of monarchy, whether by consent or force, is therefore an old form of government, especially for small states. If the state needs little administration and is not so intrusive as to necessitate large inspection, a monarchy (or patriarchy) seems to have been sufficient for administration. Abraham also refused to enter into treaties with those around him, lest he become obliged to them (Gen. 14:21-24). Treaties were already in use by 2000 BC (Gen. 21:22 ff.; 26:28). It appears, therefore, that the propriety of entering into covenanted relationships is acknowledged. The key criteria for treaties, thereafter, were religious and prudential factors. Several injunctions are is-sued to avoid treaties with parties who did not share belief in the one, true God. The basis of a treaty being either the guaranteed sufficiency of the human parties—a frail foundation—or based on an oath to God, the Lord's people should only expect treaties to be kept by those with a strong allegiance to God or some other supreme commitments.

If one questions the conventional wisdom in our country today, he may wonder why (or for what else) we might spend the amounts below as we do in foreign aid to:

- $1 billion/year to Egypt; and $5 billion to Iraq.
- Another $5 billion to Israel, Jordan, and Pakistan.
- A total of $47 billion for development and diplomacy.[43]
- Total foreign aid ranges from $37 billion (ca. 1% of the 2012 budget) to $50 billion, depending on estimates—with one recent estimate bemoaning the reduction of $61 billion in aid. (See link in the previous footnote)[44]

One of the Hebrew prophets issued a warning against "forming an alliance, not by [God's] Spirit" (Is. 30:1). Those who depend on other nations instead of God will be frustrated (Is. 30:2). God warns rulers that alliances with other nations is putting faith in the flesh instead of seeking help from the Lord (Is. 31:1-3). Modern

---

[43]   See   http://globalhealth.kff.org/Daily-Reports/2011/March/03/GH-030311-Budgets.aspx.

[44] Moreover, the Heritage Foundation reports that in UN, non-consensual voting, the recipients of billions of dollars in US Aid vote against the US 95% of the time.   http://www.heritage.org/research/reports/2010/04/us-foreign-aid-recipients-show-little-support-for-america-when-voting-at-the-united-nations.

statesmen who forget this lesson and depend on strategic alliances or treaties with unbelievers more than on the ways of God ask for the entanglements and judgments that come from such misplaced faith. To the contrary, nations must be willing to affirm: "For the Lord is our judge, the Lord is our lawgiver, the Lord is our King; it is he who will save us" (Is. 33:22). Such humility and trust in the divine graces the best of leadership. God is the "Holy One, Israel's Creator, your King" (Is. 43:15). He is also the one who establishes peace and enlarges nations (Is. 26:12-16).

Centralized Planning and Saving? Joseph's Famine (Gen. 47:13-27)

While one may be justifiably suspicious of collectivized approaches to the economy, especially in light of the rise and fall of empires in this century, nonetheless, the role of the collective in preserving grain is illustrated in Genesis 47—at least as a temporary measure. It should also be noted that this centralized plan is concerned with necessities, not "wants."

Again, one must be careful not to overreact against the excesses of recent times. Even if the majority of cases of collectivism are disastrous, one cannot on scriptural grounds rule out an exceptional or limited use of collectivist models as warranted by emergencies. It is the case, however, that such collectivist approaches are condoned only if they match conditions similar to this episode.

There is a significant difference between statist collectives and private cooperatives. Private charities have long known of economies of scale, and it is merely a wise use of resources to eliminate multiple agencies that perpetuate their own inefficiencies. One of the surest tests of the legitimacy of centralization is whether or not it is truly economical. If a task may be done more quickly or effectively by centralizing without violating any other ordained sphere, such economy is hard to fault. On the other hand, if centralization squelches humanity or violates other valid provisions, then it should be eschewed. While it would be unwise to construct the charter for a state on this model alone, yet, there may be some limited use of a co-operative in a godly model.

Taxation rates may be explored elsewhere. In the first phase of saving, Joseph used a 20% taxation rate. Later, when the famine was in full force, Joseph received money in exchange for these crops. One may question whether or not he should have received profit from what was already the people's. However, there is no evidence of protest from the people about this matter. They seemed willing to pay for the crops, when the other surrounding groups were starving. The people were paying for Joseph's industry and wise pre-planning. Twenty per cent was fair in this situation. When their money was used up, they sold their livestock and eventually pledged themselves to be Pharaoh's servants. From that time on, a 20% rate—the maximum tax rate recorded in Scripture (and that during an international emergency)—was established for whatever produce was grown (Gen. 47:26). The only tax-exemption was for the priests and their lands (Gen. 47:22, 26), a basis for tax exemption for religious charities and their essential properties.

Profit and acquisition are also present in this episode (cf. also Ex. 3:22); and this is not merely another scheme for redistribution of wealth. Joseph made a profit, and he even traded the commodity for profit, the acquisition of land, and indentured servanthood. State policies do well not to condemn the profit motive or the acquisition of personal property. All it should avoid is the unjust acquisition of such (e.g., Mk. 4:19).

As with its first occurrence in Scripture (Gen. 1:16), government in general follows the analogy of the sun and moon: they were created for specific and limited purposes by the sovereign God. As long as they conform to those purposes, they are gifts and to be honored. It is only when these luminaries escape their orbits or seek to assume another's jurisdiction that they defy God. As long as they remain submissive to the sovereign, they are useful servants. That is precisely the place of human government.

The following features of government were in existence prior to the organization of the state around the Law at Mount Sinai:

citizenship, judges, kings, treaties, chiefs, divisions, confederacies, and a prison system.

Although the above features surface (mostly among unbelieving peoples), no explicit commands are given to the state to organize or perpetuate these functions. On the contrary, the following aspects of human existence were assigned strictly to the family at this early period: marriage, worship, inheritance, agriculture, commerce, education, justice, defense (military engagements), and environment.

Amidst such evolution, however, the family was still the primary unit of government. There is wisdom (although slightly overstated) in John Frame's view that, "state authority is essentially family authority and extended somewhat by the demands of number and geography."[45] While one might not state the authority as baldly as Frame, nevertheless, it is imperative to realize that the family is more basic than the state. That conclusion is heartily endorsed throughout Scripture.

The state should not interfere with these tasks assigned to the family except in an extreme emergency and with compelling concern for the good of all. It must be kept in its lawful place.

The sum of Biblical Foundations thus far may be comprehended under the enduring and important subjects of:

(1) Revelation: Listen to it.

(2) Spheres and Divisions of Governments: know these and refer policy matters to the appropriate sphere.

(3) Family: it is still the cellular base of politics.

(4) The Fall affects us more than most policy studies or political platforms know.

(5) The whole counsel of God is desperately needed as we question conventional notions. In short, questioning politics will pose at least these questions to political matters before us in all ages.

---

[45] John Frame, "Toward a Theology of the State," op. cit., 217. By such logic, Frame also rules out Lutheran views, Meredith Kline's intrusion ethic, and the Anabaptist view that sees the state as essentially Satanic.

My answer to the main Question of chapter 1 is this: In view of the Fall of mankind and the need to limit governments, Build Strong families and stronger churches!

Chapter 2

What Happens When Governments Grow Too Large?

The 1960s and 1970s in America witnessed an explosion in immorality, simultaneous with an expansion of the scope of the government. By the later 1980s, government took 36.8% of the nation's product[46]—a rate that would rise to approximately 40% by the mid-1990s. While illegitimacy ratios were exploding, at the same time the number of federal employees also grew at an astronomical rate. Following the expansion of the state under the New Deal, federal employees in Washington rose from 75,000 in 1933 to 166,000 in 1940. In 1933, each member of Congress was permitted to hire only two staff members, but over the next half century, U.S. House and Senate staffs boomed from 1,425 in 1930 to 6,255 in 1960 to 10,739 in 1970.[47] Emblematic of this eruption, the U.S. Department of State had 6,438 employees in 1940, 25,380 in 1950, and 39,603 in 1970. Kevin Phillips reports that by 1970 this expansion, "had raised the number of federal employees in

---

[46] Doug Bandow, *Beyond Good Intentions* (Westchester, IL: Crossway, 1988), 81.

[47] Kevin Phillips, *Arrogant Capital* (Boston: Little, Brown and Co., 1994), 24-25.

metropolitan Washington to 327,000, up from 223,000 in 1950 and 73,000 in 1930."[48] Federal employment grew to assume oversight responsibility for what amounted to one-third of the national economy, with 2.1 million civilian employees and 1.9 million military employees. In contrast to the slimmer governments of earlier days, by the 1990s 1.5 trillion dollars per year were exchanged by 135 federal agencies. Although causal relationships are difficult to prove, it seemed as if a culture that had once maintained at least implicit religious groundings was placing its energy and capital elsewhere. The replacement was a larger governmental bureaucracy that simultaneously yielded more humanism and less theism.

Federal employees in the American government tripled from 1940 (700,000) to 1970, hitting 2.2 million employees. During the 1970s, 80s, and 90s, federal employees remained almost constant, with a slight decrease by 2000.[49] The total number of government employees over the past decade has grown substantially, in part due to a massive expansion related to the Homeland Security Department.

However by early 2010, the *Washington Post* (Feb. 2, 2010) heralded that, "The era of big government has returned with a vengeance, in the form of the largest federal work force in modern history. The Obama administration says the government will grow to 2.15 million employees this year, topping 2 million for the first time since President Clinton declared that 'the era of big government is over' and joined forces with a Republican-led Congress in the 1990s to pare back the federal work force." Some estimates put the number of federal employees at almost 2.8 million,[50] while New York University professor Paul Light calculates that the true size of government employment is 14.6 million people, if one includes postal and military employees.[51]

---

[48] Ibid., 26.

[49] Source: http://www.opm.gov/feddata/HistoricalTables/Executive-BranchSince1940.asp.

[50] Source: http://www.numberof.net/number-of-federal-employees-2/.

[51] That study, which surveys employment since 1962, may be found at: http://tinyurl.com/yaak7na.

Moreover, if state and local government employees are added (even without the military), almost 20 million Americans are employed by the government.[52] While in some respects for a long period of time (since 1946), federal employees peaked and stabilized, local government employees and state government employees increased four-fold and five-fold respectively during the same half century.[53]

Similarly, it is time to ask: What happens when governments grow too large? Can a government be so expansive that it cripples incentive, responsibility, or morality? Or is bigger always and automatically better? Would a perspective from a larger distance and non-secular knowledge-base provide guidance? This chapter addresses those questions, even if that is an unconventional position, primarily by reviewing several key passages from the Hebrew Old Testament.

Biblical Examples of Informed Politics: this is not new

The Bible provides an early pattern for a representative form of government in Exodus 18. A seventeenth century political theorist, Johannes Althusius, extolled: "I consider that no polity from the beginning of the world has been more wisely and perfectly constructed than the polity of the Jews. We err, I believe, whenever in similar circumstances we depart from it." Part of what he had in mind as unimproveable was an early form of republican-federal government. American Christians would do well to review the origins of our own form of government to realize its biblical moorings. I wish to highlight the following:

Proposition: The government laid down in the Scriptures is the best source for human government.

Corollary: The best form of government comes from the mind of God, not the management of man.

Many Christians do not imagine that the Bible has very much to tell our government, our governors, and the governed. Many

---

[52] Source: http://www.date.360.org/dsg.aspx?Data_Set_Group_Id=228.

[53] Source: http://www.date.360.org/dsg.aspx?Data_Set_Group_Id=228.

Christians also believe that the Bible is more piously-minded than to bother itself with mundane matters like politics. Admittedly, biblical statements on matters of government rarely produce goose bumps or laughing revivals. However, the Bible's information and instructions on matters of civil government are equally matters of revelation, as are its statements pertaining to salvation, social responsibility, prayer, or providence.

The heart of biblical order is the belief that sinful minds, apart from the special revelation of God, will not automatically conceive correct structures. Hence, as an act of his mercy much like his revelation in the law, God gives to his people that which they would not concoct on their own. In his mercy, he spares not only eternal lostness, but also some measure of temporal lostness by obviating the need to search for sound organizational principles and structures. Instead of abandoning his creation to the futility of Sisyphus, God reveals the basic pattern of government for his people. He did not leave Christians in the dark. The regular life and ordering of the state is far too important, at least to God, to leave to caprice, to the shifting sands of corporate culture, or to human ingenuity. Such revelation from God on political matters is a token of God's grace, wisdom, and providence.

For those who value organizational efficiency, it is not necessary to "re-invent the wheel." The biblical aspects of government need not be ignored by each successive generation, nor rediscovered by alternating generations. One could profit much by studying the "old paths" (Jer. 6:16, 18:15) and by attempting to mold governments after the patterns of spiritual ancestors. That, far from being a pharisaic expression of traditionalism, is the better part of wisdom in the search to rule out inefficient modes of governing. History has heuristic value in helping to eliminate erroneous dead-end paths and ineffective nostrums.

Specifically, Exodus 18 (Jethro and Moses) provides an early example of federal-republican structure, which became the basis for our American republic. That is to assert that our government structure is inherently and originally religious in nature and root.

The best government follows and models the best government in the Bible.

During a severe famine in the 19th century BC, the Israelites went down to Egypt under Joseph's nurture. At first, Israel's sons were part of the ruling class, but when a new Egyptian dynasty arose (Ex. 1:8), the Israelites were subjected to slavery (Ex. 1:12-14). The oppression of the Jews grew under this repressive monarchy until God raised up a deliverer: Moses.

A reluctant revolutionary, Moses demonstrated the superiority of God over Pharaoh by ten plagues, the last of which cost Pharaoh his first-born son. Finally, the Israelites were allowed to leave Egypt and return to form their own nation-state. Although Pharaoh pursued, God protected these people, but they continued to rebel. Their rebellion resulted in a generation-long wandering in the Sinai wilderness. The spirit of rebelliousness against God's authority necessarily had to be extinguished before Israel could begin to possess their land. Still, even in this wilderness, God was preparing Moses and the people for the Republic of Israel.

During the time of Moses and Pharaoh, there was a consistent tradition of governmental structure. In the earliest of times, small units were governed by patriarchs or elders. As time and culture progressed, and as human leaders began to aspire to higher levels of power, the earliest nations came into existence (e. g., Gen. 10). These early nations adopted a convention that both has value and also has great potential for abuse: monarchy. Algernon Sydney suggested that Nimrod was the first monarch (see Gen. 10), beginning a tradition in violence and arrogance. What may have been a deviation from God's original plan, persisted until the time of Moses. In between Nimrod and Moses, the notion of a republic vanished or seemed unknown. The donation of a republican structure to the world would await the divine revelation through a non-Israeli.

A century before Moses, still most governments were either small tribal units, or if large, monarchies. The pinnacle of Egyptian culture saw monarch after monarch follow one another in dynastic succession. The great Pharaohs – Rameses, Thutmoses, and Tutankhamon – were authoritarian monarchs, pure and simple. In the half century preceding Moses, there were no institutions like the senate, a council, no other checking branches of government. Unilateral power was located in the monarch, both in the Middle East and the Far East.

Moreover, all that the people of Israel knew – four centuries after the time of Jacob – was the monarchical pattern of government. They had no other ideas or notions about government, other than the hierarchical form. Other schemes were forgotten, unknown, or at least not practiced anywhere around them. Thus, the republican-type plan suggested by Jethro comes as such an innovation and did not have its origin in the mind of man or the will of the flesh.

Jethro's Republic

In Exodus 18, Jethro is introduced as "the priest of Midian and father-in-law of Moses." Earlier (Ex. 2:18), Moses' father-in-law had been called "Reuel." Rather than viewing this as in inherent contradiction within the pages of Scripture, one of two solutions provides a harmony. When Exodus 2:21 speaks of Reuel as giving his daughter (Zipporah) in marriage to Moses, linguistically it is possible that Zipporah was the niece or granddaughter of Reuel, the term "father" used of him in the sense of patriarch or head of the extended family. Under that construction, Reuel would be the grandfather or great uncle of Zipporah, with Jethro being her father and Moses' father-in-law. That is one linguistic possibility.

A more likely explanation is that Reuel was the family name, surname, or nick-name of Jethro. Frequently, biblical characters were known by several names (Jacob-Israel, Peter-Cephas, Daniel-Belteshazzar). That being the case, it is difficult to believe that the Bible would be so mindless as to contradict itself within the span of a few short verses, when this character is called "Reuel" in Exodus 2:18, and only eight verses later (Ex. 3:1) is called "Jethro, his father-in-law, the priest of Midian." Thus, most commentators sympathetic to the authenticity of Scripture, understand these two names to refer to the same person.

As early as Exodus 3:1, therefore, we see a priest who is of non-Israeli origin – one of the many cases of God using and dwelling in others than Israelites in the OT. Jethro was either a member/priest of a false cult, deserving, according to the Mosaic legislation, death as a false prophet and idolater; or he was a pre-Israeli believer. He certainly was not a Muslim, a Hindu, a pantheist, or a polytheist. He seemed to worship and serve the true God. Contrary to some ideas, God did not work exclusively with or through Jews in the OT. Jethro, as we shall see, was quite mature and spiritually minded; so much so that in Exodus 18 he served as a spiritual mentor to Moses.

Following the exodus from Egypt, Jethro hears the good report. As any parent, he is anxious to reunite his daughter's family. During the critical period leading up to the Exodus, evidently Moses sent Zipporah and his two sons (Gershom and Eliezer) to remain in Jethro's safe-keeping (Ex. 18:2-4) – another indication that Jethro was not a priest in a false cult. Moses would hardly resort to idolatrous supervision of his wife and sons if Jethro had been so evil. The presumption of the narrative, therefore, is that Jethro is on the side of God. His subsequent insight and advice seems to confirm that.

Jethro heard what "God had done for Moses and for his people Israel, and how the Lord had brought Israel out of Egypt." (Ex. 18:1) Accordingly, as soon as possible, Jethro, Zipporah, and Moses' sons travel to meet him in the desert (Ex. 18:5). To observe something of the respect Moses had for Jethro, one may note that it was Moses who went out to greet his father-in-law (18:7), not vice-versa. Moreover, Moses "bowed down and kissed him," certainly a sign of respect and admiration unexpected for an idolater. After these initial greetings, they conversed and counseled one another about "everything the Lord had done to Pharaoh . . . and how the Lord had saved them." (Ex. 18:8) Such spiritual conversation was fitting for fellow-believers. Indeed, Jethro's reaction to these reports further evidences his since faith: "Jethro was delighted to hear about all the good things the Lord had done for Israel in rescuing them from the hand of the Egyptians." (18:9) He praised the Lord and acknowledged God as the true rescuer of Israel (18:10). He confessed emphatically ("Now I *know*") that "the Lord is greater than all other gods, for he did this to those who had treated Israel arrogantly." (18:11). These sincere affirmations and expressions of praise are climaxed with a sacrificial feast – never condemned in the slightest by Moses nor by God himself. Jethro, not Moses, offers a burnt offering and sacrifice to God, and Aaron and the elders join in the feast "with Moses' father-in-law in the presence of God." (18:12) This was no pagan feast; it was one celebrated by those who knew God best. In this case, Jethro was perhaps more spiritually advanced than even Moses.

Jethro observed and proceeded to make other recommendations. The following day, Jethro observed Moses acting as judge for the people. He listened to their cases from morning till evening. No one else shared in the government with him. Even though gifted and well-meaning, Jethro had the spiritual insight to suggest a better method of governance – an early republican model. He told Moses (v. 14) that what he was doing was not right: "Why do you alone sit as judge?" Moses gave an answer, but Jethro replied: "What you are doing is not good. You and these people who come to you will only wear yourselves out. The work is too heavy for you; you cannot handle it alone. Listen now to me and I will give you some advice, and may God be with you. You must be the people's representative before God and bring their disputes to him. Teach them the decrees and laws, and show them the way to live and the duties they are to perform. But select capable men from all the people, men who fear God, trustworthy men who hate dishonest gain, and appoint them as officials over thousands, hundreds, fifties, and tens. Have them serve as judges for the people at all times, but have them bring every difficult case to you; the simple cases they can decide themselves. . . . If you do this and God so commands, you will be able to stand the strain, and all these people will go home satisfied." (Ex. 18:17-25)

A form of governing is introduced during Moses' leadership.

The presence of elders as community leaders is apparent from early times (Ex. 3:16; 4:29). Rather than instituting either a democracy or a monarchy, God raises up a plurality of mature, prudent representative leaders. They are to have wisdom, the fear of the Lord, trustworthiness, and hatred of graft (Ex. 18:21). This early form of a representative government indicates that layers of accountability (Ex. 18:21) are warranted, with differing levels of leadership hearing appeals and acting on matters as they arise (Dt. 1:15-18). In contrast to the predominance of monarchs at the time, Jethro did not advocate a monarchy. Instead, he advised Moses to institute a graduated series of administrations. This early pattern permits problems to be handled first by those closest to the issues. Then, if not satisfactory, they may proceed to the next level of administration (appeal). Both church and state share this feature in their best governmental manifestations. This federal structure preserves a blend of grass-rootedness with a modicum of unity. The earliest American constitutional documents sought to preserve and perpetuate this delicate balance between unity and independence. It seems that the earliest republican form of government came from the mind of God, through Jethro, a non-Israeli priest, long before either the Golden Age of Greco-Roman governance or the Enlightenment or modern revolutions.

This seemed obvious to those in the founding era of America. Samuel Langdon (1788), for example, commented about the Mosaic period: "Thus a senate was evidently constituted, as necessary for the future government of the nation, under a chief commander. And as to the choice of this senate, doubtless the people were consulted, who appear to have had a voice in all public affairs from time to time, the whole congregation being called together on all important occasions: the government therefore was a proper republic." He proceeded to state the value of the judicial laws of Moses:

> A government, thus settled on republican principles, required laws; without which it must have degenerated immediately into aristocracy, or absolute monarchy. But God did not leave a people, wholly unskilled in legislation, to make laws for themselves: he

took this important matter wholly into his own hands, and beside the moral laws of the two tables, which directed their conduct as individuals, gave them by Moses a complete code of judicial laws. They were not numerous indeed, but concise and plain, and easily applicable to almost every controversy which might arise between man and man, and every criminal case which might require the judgment of the court. Of these some were peculiarly adapted to their national form, as divided into tribes and families always to be kept distinct; others were especially suited to the peculiar nature of the government as a theocracy, God himself being eminently their king, and manifesting himself among them in a visible manner, by the cloud of glory in the tabernacle and temple. This was the reason why blasphemy, and all obstinate disobedience to his laws, were considered as high treason, and punished with death; especially idolatry, as being a crime against the fundamental principles of the constitution. But far the greater part of the judicial laws were founded on the plain immutable principles of reason, justice, and social virtue; such as are always necessary for civil society.[54]

Many theorists, ranging from Aquinas and Machiavelli to Althusius and Thielicke, see Jethro's advice as a pristine example of federalism or republicanism. Commenting on the parallel passage in Deuteronomy 1:14-16, John Calvin stated: "Hence it more plainly appears that those who were to preside in judgment were not appointed only by the will of Moses, but elected by the votes of the people. And this is the most desirable kind of liberty, that we should not be compelled to obey every person who may be tyrannically put over our heads; but which allows of election, so that no one should rule except he be approved by us. And this is further confirmed in the next verse, wherein Moses recounts that he awaited the consent of the people, and that nothing was attempted which did not please them all." Thus, Calvin viewed this as a representative republican form.

Thomas Aquinas is accurately understood as advocating a constitutional monarchy synthesized with certain democratical

---

[54] This sermon is contained in my *Election Day Sermons* (Oak Ridge, TN: The Kuyper Institute, 1996).

elements. For the best ordering of the state, the form of government should combine the best of various forms:

> Accordingly, the best form of government is in a state or kingdom, wherein one is given the power to preside over all; while under him are others having governing powers: and yet a government of this kind is shared by all, both because all are eligible to govern, and because the rulers are chosen by all. For this is the best form of polity, being partly kingdom, since there is one at the head of all; partly aristocracy, in so far as a number of persons are set in authority; partly democracy, i.e., government by the people, in so far as the rulers can be chosen from the people, and the people have the right to choose their rulers.[55]

Aquinas viewed the Mosaic government as an early incarnation of democracy: "Such was the form of government established by the Divine Law. For Moses and his successors governed the people in such a way that each of them was ruler over all . . . Moreover, seventy-two men were chosen, who were elders in virtue . . . so that there was an element of aristocracy. But it was a democratical government in so far as the rulers were chosen from all the people . . ."[56]

Other biblical commentators have interpreted similarly. In his first chapter, Althusius, who thought the Mosaic government to be quite adequate, noted that the first table of the law regulated true piety, while the second addressed true justice: "In the former, everything is to be referred immediately to the glory of God; in the latter, to the utility and welfare of the people associated in one body. These are the two foundations of every good association. Whenever a turning away from them has begun, the happiness of a realm or universal association is diminished."

Althusius frequently iterated that "piety is required by the first table of the Decalogue and justice by the second, and the two together are furthermore validated in human experience everywhere." In the Preface to a 1614 (3rd) edition, Althusius

---

[55] Thomas Aquinas, *Summa Theologica*, 2nd edition (London: Burns Oates& Wahbourne Ltd., 1921), Q 105, Art. 1.
[56] Thomas Aquinas, *Summa Theologica*, Q 105, Art. 1.

stated: "I have included among other things herein, all in their proper places, the precepts of the Decalogue and the rights of sovereignty, about which there is a deep silence among some other political scientists. The precepts of the Decalogue are included to the extent that they infuse a vital spirit into the association and symbiotic life that we teach, that they carry a torch before the social life that we seek, and that they prescribe and constitute a way, rule, guiding star, and boundary for human society. If anyone would take them out of politics, he would destroy it; indeed, he would destroy all symbiosis and social life among men."[57]

The government that values wisdom and longevity will neither despise nor overlook these values that provide the essential foundation for various policies and laws. The early republics established by God were suitable for modern imitation. In earlier republics, an outline of such duties gave clear guidance for the place of government.

So we are not the first, nor the last, to see the value of this early republican form. Even Machiavelli, often perceived as the arch-enemy of righteousness, spoke favorably of the Mosaic government. (*The Prince*, 20, 22, 85; *Discourses*, 133)

The result was that Moses listened, obeyed, and benefited from this advice (18:24-25). He chose qualified men and assigned them various jurisdictions, with the possibility of appeal to the higher structure if justice was not satisfied. This is the origin of the federal or republican form of government – one that was led by representatives and contained correction for maladministration.

With no other prior examples, and with this innovation coming from a spiritual man, the question below almost begs itself:

What was the origin of this idea, since it was so unusual? God.
Since this pattern can hardly be ascribed to the surrounding nations or to earlier precedent, and since it is not the most efficient form of government, the origin of the idea of republicanism may be inexplicable apart from divine revelation. Indeed, no ruling

---

[57] Johannes Althusius, *Politica* (1603, rpr. Indianapolis: Liberty Fund, 1995), 11-12.

class – apart from thoroughly religious virtue – would dream up such power sharing. Nor would any but people most distrustful of leadership concoct such balance of power. It seems that the only likely explanations for the origin of this republicanism lie in (1) the divine revelation from God through Jethro, or (2) the logical extension of the doctrine of human depravity. Of course, these two together provide a satisfactory rationale for the beginning of republican government.

That being the case, we affirm that the mind of God is both clear and gracious in providing such form of government and patterns of organization for us. Five specifics may be drawn from this first model.

First, these teachings call into question other governmental structures. If the republic is God's preferred pattern in most cases, strong justification must be made if one does not follow that model.

Second, all these structures show the wisdom and kindness of God. He is not a God who is merely concerned with how we live in the after life. He cares about our well-being in the here and now. And he gives us plenty of information how to guide, improve, and sustain a government. God is not a gnostic.

Third, this proves that Scripture is a comprehensive book, not focused only on a small slice of life. God wants to give his people a comprehensive world view. It is just all too often the case that his people try to restrict it or simplify it. Scripture does not have a small scope; it speaks to many areas.

Fourth, these patterns reinforce that the wisdom of God is greater than plan of man. Why re-invent government when we already have a timeless pattern?

Finally, this form takes into account other theological teachings (e.g., human depravity). It also reminds us that no individual, not even Moses, is sufficient to do all tasks. We must not expect nor allow governors to attempt every task.

Therefore, governments have been constructed with checks and balances, the best of which provide for regular and thoughtful means of accountability. Most Christians acknowledge that to achieve this, constitutions must follow the faithful patterns of God.

Such constitutions serve to delimit unbridled subjectivity and will-reign, exhibiting a firm belief in the need to limit the power of any individual.

Hence, constitutionalism fosters a restraint on sin. It is sin, however, that demands a resulting form of government. Our theology of sin and our anthropology are the values that shape our consequent civil government. Theology thus molds polity. That is one answer for questioning politics. One may also ask what other insights the OT may yield for political wisdom.

An Ancient Office: Judges

At times throughout history, the Lord would raise up various armies to humble his people (Jud. 2:14) and draw their attention back to himself. God viewed the covenant with Israel as "violated," and he decreed to use them to test Israel" (Jud. 2:22). Both testaments present God as the true Sovereign over military affairs and over the development of nations. Further, "the Lord allowed those nations to remain; he did not drive them out at once by giving them into the hands" of Israel (Jud. 2:23). God both permits and drives out. Judges 3:3 recounts the nations which he sovereignly allowed to test Israel, and also explains that his purpose was to teach Israel how to engage in warfare (Jud. 3:2).

During the period of the Judges, God raised up a diversity of leaders, and not all were righteous in all their ways. The judges, however, are seldom observed in actual judicial capacity. Thus, there is little biblical basis for an institution which conjoins the judicial and royal power. During times of good leadership, the nation would thrive (Jud. 2:18), while the tendency toward degeneration persisted toward the end of this administration. Accordingly, there was also a cumulative trend toward increased corruption and oppression (Jud. 2:19).

Several judges were quite violent, such as Ehud. While it would not be safe to universalize from his assassination, it should be recognized that during extreme situations, sometimes extreme measures are needed. Deborah, as a judge of Israel at the time, models the leadership role that women may have in government. Although there is prohibition of women serving as elders in the church (1 Tim. 2:11-12), the same prohibition did not apply to women serving in the state. Deborah served effectively, bravely, and with good wisdom. It is also possible that when males fail to do their duty with bravery, God will raise up women to perform the tasks (cf. Jud. 4:17-21).

It is evidently appropriate to sing praises to God for military victory (Jud. 5). "Princes" led in the victory, and "kings" and "rulers" are warned to submit to God. Deborah sang perceptively: "When they chose new gods, war came to the city gates" (Jud. 5:8), a reflection of the impact of theology on the security of the state. Other serenaders will recite the righteous acts of the Lord and "the righteous acts of his warriors" (Jud. 5:10).

Even though other states had kings who came and fought against Israel (Jud. 5:19), God the Sovereign Commander was working behind the scenes. The Angel of the Lord uttered a curse on those who did not stand with the Lord (Jud. 5:23), and many since that time have understood that to be a continuing principle.[58]

Gideon is another example of violent resistance. By his example, he also legitimizes tactics such as: sneak attacks, military disinformation, the use of special troops, and the use of surprise. Gideon was also faithful to his orders to kill the opposing leaders (Jud. 8:21). A quite interesting feature of his reign was that when he was petitioned to establish a monarchy (which would eventually occur several centuries later), he declined. The lack of *hubris* in Gideon—especially when it is noted how popular he was—is a trait worthy of imitation. The people requested Gideon to establish a hereditary monarchy (Jud. 8:22). He refused, and further ordered that his son (who was either too young or had shown a lack of

---

[58] To sense something of the continuing relevance of this passage, one might recall the mid-seventeenth century sermon to the British Parliament based on this text by Stephen Marshall, an outstanding preacher in London. Among his applications from *Meroz Cursed,* were that the civil leaders were to "Come to the help of the Lord" and his people. All who stood with God's people were blessed, and those who did not help were cursed like Meroz. More modern applications, no doubt, could also be made.

courage) would not rule over them either. In lieu of that honor, Gideon did, however, accept a large tribute that he smelted into a monument. As soon as the monument was completed, the people "prostituted themselves by worshipping it there." Even selfless leaders may be unable to quench the inordinate and evil desires of people.

After Gideon's death, Abimelech assassinated the 70 sons (princes) of Gideon. It is apparent that early on there were kings, governors (Jud. 9:30), and princes. It is also apparent that citizens' loyalty may be quite fickle (Jud. 9:23). When they take things into their own hands, normally more violence and immorality result (Jud. 9:25). Violence among political leaders seems to beget more violence (Jud. 9: 46-49, 53).

Throughout the era of the judges, elders also functioned, showing the continuity of that presbyterian form of government (Jud. 11:5, 10). Samson led the people for twenty years and was less than upright much of the time. Still, while in a Philistinian prison, he wrought revenge for the Lord. The Book of Judges illustrates the results of a corrupt government and religion. The two seem to go together frequently. The great immorality in Judges 19 reveals the true end of the logic of individualism. When every man does what is right in his own eyes, society decomposes. Legal or political reform, apart from moral reformation and renovation, will seldom have lasting effects.

With its genesis in Moses's day—complete with layers of original and appellate jurisdiction (Ex. 18)—this office reached its zenith in the Book of Judges. Some of the great judges i. e., Othniel, Ehud, Gideon, Jephthah, Samson, were religious-civic leaders who led the people when "every man did right in his own eyes." These "judges" who led the Israelis from about 1300-1050 BC were the political leaders until Saul became the first king. One may also remember that God thought that a judge-ocracy was an acceptable form of government. The *people* (*demos*) of Israel—not God—thought that they should have a monarch. Two-hundred years later, Jehoshaphat sees the failure of that humanly-engineered form of government and seeks to return to the form which God initiated.

When Jehoshaphat reinstituted the "judges," he was harking back to an erstwhile pattern and seeking to return to God's ways and not man's ways.

Israel's First Monarch: 1 Samuel

Scripture is not exclusively concerned with the spiritual; it also treats the physical mechanisms that convey the spiritual. In studying the proper scope of the state, a maxim becomes clear: the *role* of the state is practically inseparable from the issues and *rulers* of the state. The practitioners of statecraft lead the state. The Bible does not provide barren theory about the role of the state alone; it also exhibits good and bad statecraft. Besides describing the developments of the Israeli monarchy, this chapter also highlights some of the good and bad statecraft for a period of nearly 500 years. This compendium of revealed politics can benefit any who assess various leaders and forms of the state.[59]

Samuel was the last of the great Judges, leading in approximately 1080 BC. Although Samuel is referred to as a "prophet," he was also a political leader, a Judge (1 Sam. 7:15-17). He acted in judicial capacity throughout Israel and sought to appoint his own sons as judges (1 Sam. 8:1). However, they were unfit. The nation of Israel was surrounded by pagan neighbors and fell into the seduction of wanting to be "like" others. The aspiration to be like another power is at the heart of the Fall of angels (Is. 14:13-14), the Fall of humans, and the fall of nations. Israel, as a nation, and any nation faces this danger, falls if it attempts to imitate other nations' government in place of God's government.

Israel assessed how other nations ordered their business and politics. Their observation was that all the other nations had a king. Monarchy was a novelty (so they argued) in political organization. It was their opinion that such a monarchy would be a political panacea. The people aspired to remedy their situation with a

---

[59] For a historic and helpful discussion of the unfolding of the Israelite monarchy, cf. Junius Brutus, *A Defense of Liberty Against Tyrants*, trans. Harold J. Laski (Gloucester, MA: Peter Smith, 1963), 71-128.

political tool. They hoped for political salvation, when the real solution for their emergency was a renewed dependence on the Kingship of God—not the kingship of man. David Payne observes: "No nation has ever found some magical constitutional formula to solve every social and political problem; but a people that seeks above all to honor and obey God possesses . . . stability and serenity which allow it to confront universal and permanent problems with both courage and compassion, and with a considerable measure of success."[60]

These Israelites "wanted a king, because they imagined that Jehovah their God-King was not able to secure their constant prosperity."[61] Christians should learn from this *not* to expect that some political reorganization or new structure will work out real societal problems. Real problems need real solutions—not smoke-and-mirrors political masking. In this case, rather than seeking a new monarchical form of government, Israel should have deepened their practice of theocracy, the rule of God. They should have strengthened their adherence to the Kingship of God instead of rejecting the sovereignty of Jahweh (cf. 1 Sam. 8:7 & 10:19) and embracing the kingship of man.

First Samuel 8 describes their request. Toward the end of Samuel's life, the people came to ask him to "appoint a king to lead us, such as all the other nations have." The driving motivation for the change in forms of leadership was the desire to conform to the practice of the surrounding nations. History documents political changes that seek to be in step with all the other trends at the expense of obedience to God. International political peer pressure is not a reason to change forms of leadership *simply* because all the other groups of nations adopt a particular form.

If leadership structure can be improved by superior forms of organization, then nations should benefit. However, they should be careful not to change merely because others introduce new patterns

---

[60] David Payne, *The Daily Study Bible: I & II Samuel* (Philadelphia: Westminster, 1982), 40-41.

[61] Carl Keil and Franz Delitzsch, *Commentary on the Old Testament* (rpr. Grand Rapids: Eerdmans, 1978), vol. 2, 84.

of leadership. Further, the people blatantly admitted their motive: "Then we will be like all the other nations, with a king to lead us and to go out before us and fight our battles" (1 Samuel 8:20).

Their hope was that a monarchy would bring stability and military prowess to Israel. They blamed the defects of their national life on the political *form*, not recognizing that their sin, their moral deficiency, and their lack of adherence to the Monarchy of God were the roots of their problem. Changes of form will not cure moral defect or decay; at best, governmental form may limit human ills. Government is not therapeutic.

Israel may have blinded herself to the fact that the monarchy would have some problems in it. They were so enamored with an idea and in such haste to have a king who would do the difficult work for them that they rushed headlong over the cliff of the latest political science. Periodically, other nations or groups diminish their responsibility in similar ways. With regularity, believers ought to recommit themselves to avoiding quick-fixes by strengthening their commitment to work out their national problems, instead of looking for utopian political leaders or solutions.

Unfortunately, sometimes people will embrace any kind of leadership, if that leadership change offers utopian promises even if it means abandoning centuries of good patterns. Often it seems that states will surrender precious matters in exchange for a political leader who promises to take away pressing difficulties. People who rely on someone else to take away their problems for them do so at the cost of sacrificing liberty. Christians guided by these OT principles should be particularly sensitive to this tendency.

In 1 Samuel 8:10 ff., God gave Samuel predictions about what would certainly happen if Israel instituted a monarchy. The people were thinking about what a king would *give* to the nation, but Samuel warned them about what a king would *take* from the nation. In verse eleven, he warned that the king will conscript the sons and draft them into the army. The citizens will have little input over what tasks they are assigned (12). The daughters will also be drafted to work for the state (13). The king will *take* a cut of the best fields and vineyards (14). He will also help himself to a tenth of the grain and give that to his administration (15).[62] He will *seize* other assets (16) and the flocks; and the people will become his slaves (17). These are some of the attendant dangers of a human monarchy. When these occur, Samuel warned, "you will cry out for relief from the king you have chosen, and the Lord will not answer you in that day" (18).

Tragically, all that Samuel foretold about the monarch and his abuse of power would be fulfilled in Saul. Toward the end of Samuel's life he was permitted to observe the sad prophecies of Saul's plight coming true.

Governing by Usurpation: Leaders Grasping too much

Saul became a corrupt ruler. The first sign of this was his overstepping of the official prerogative, arrogating unto himself the priestly duties of offering sacrifice. In 1 Samuel 13:13ff., Saul overstepped his jurisdiction in a fatal way. The office of king was not to be confused with the office of priest. Even a monarchy manifests a series of checks-and-balances and a division of labor. It is not God's style of government to set one man up as the sole authority without other checks. Unfortunately, Saul grew impatient, or Samuel was late, or Saul purposely exceeded his bounds and offered up the burnt offering (13:9). Eventually, Samuel arrived and soundly rebuked Saul for acting foolishly and disobeying the Lord (13:13-14).

One of the perennial errors of leadership is the usurpation of others' jurisdiction. This overstepping of jurisdiction may occur in the church, in the school, and frequently recurs in the modern state. It is a serious flaw to seek to extend leadership where it is not divinely warranted. Even today the modern "king," the state, sometimes seems to make unwarranted excursions into the territory of the priesthood.

---

[62] 1 Samuel 17:25 demonstrates that taxes were levied by this time. Interpreters, however, differ on whether or not this passage represents 10% as an oppressive rate. Some believe that it is the *amount* itself which is excessive (although there is little explicit biblical evidence supporting Israeli taxation prior to this); others construe that it was not so much the high rate that was wrong but the confiscatory, unjust, and possessive *nature* of the taxation.

Saul was guilty of usurping Samuel's priestly role. This was caused both by his impatience and lack of faith and by his decreasing humility. There is little worse than overweening, proud leaders who think they can provide total service for all needs. Leadership is not to be totalitarian, rather it is to be responsible, fair, and merciful within its own jurisdiction and limits. Leaders, political and otherwise, must respect the sphere sovereignty[63] of other areas. Only God can provide for all things, and only God has no limits on his leadership. Human leaders who seek to imitate God's providence or his infinity are idolatrous. Respect for jurisdiction of responsibility is essential for a godly society.

Leaders must not overstep their lawful bounds; they must be kept in check to prevent the usurping of another's jurisdiction. God does not sanction any totalitarian structure, nor any individual remaining unchecked. There are limits imposed by God on every human leader.

Monarchy, however, is not disqualified by God as a form of government. In fact, God purposely chose that metaphor to speak of Christ, who is often depicted as a king. Many are impoverished by ignorance about the Kingship of Christ. Of course, no human king can save. Royalty, itself can never secure salvation, unless the Occupant of the throne is the Divine Savior.

Christ is a coronated King, after all. His Majesty, King Jesus, the only perfect King (1 Tim. 6:13), is our Governor—more than a mere President or Chairman. Of the increase of his government (Is. 9:7), there shall be no end and this Lord of Lords and King of Kings, Jesus Christ, shall reign forever and ever (Rev. 11:15).

Even though Saul was a wicked king, monarchy is upheld by God and ordered upheld by the people. Because of his persistent disobedience, Saul was ultimately repudiated by God. God had authorized battles, including the elimination of rival kings in warfare, but Saul thought it was better to spare their lives and keep the best of the bounty (1 Sam. 15:8-10). The Lord rejected Saul

---

[63] This term is taken from Herman Dooyeweerd, *New Critique of Theoretical Thought* (Nutley, NJ: Presbyterian and Reformed, 1969). It is also summarized in his *The Christian Idea of the State* (Nutley, NJ: Craig Press, 1968).

because he did not obey the divine instructions (1 Sam. 15:11). David is then anointed as his replacement by Samuel (1 Sam. 16).

David's life prior to becoming king provides an interesting example of respecting a corrupt ruler. Among King David's fine traits were his submission to Saul, even when King Saul tried to murder him. So great was David's respect for God and his providential government that he would not rebel against even a wicked king (1 Sam. 26). On this occasion, one of David's lieutenants, Abishai, volunteered to assassinate the ruler for him (1 Sam. 26:8). However, David responded: "Don't destroy him! Who can lay a hand on the Lord's anointed and be guiltless . . . But the Lord forbid that I should lay a hand on the Lord's anointed" (1 Sam. 26:9, 11). Moreover, David was so respectful of the office of king that he proceeded to rebuke Saul's guards for their lack of security (1 Sam. 15-16). Saul had repeatedly attempted to kill David, but each time David refused to retaliate against the divinely-anointed king. David had several tempting opportunities to assassinate Saul, but conscientiously refrained each time. Christians living under the rule of an evil king must take this into account and not easily rebel against the providence of God.

Political Poetry

Psalm 33 extols God's sovereignty: "The Lord foils the plans of the nations; he thwarts the purposes of the peoples. But the plans of the Lord stand firm forever" (vss. 10-11). Since God is the ultimate Sovereign, those nations who follow him are blessed (Ps. 33:12). Despite external shows of force, "No king is saved by the size of his army; no warrior escapes by his great strength" (Ps. 33:16). Even the most reliable of military weaponry and earthly prowess will not protect a king who is targeted by God for ousting.

In *Psalm 45* (a wedding song written for a king), the king is praised and commended for his military conquests (45:3-5). Amidst these accolades for the earthly king, the Psalmist lapses into praise for God as King: "Your throne, O God, will last forever and ever; a scepter of justice will be the scepter of your kingdom" (Ps. 45:6).

Again, God's kingship is affirmed as an everlasting and ever-just reign.

Psalm 72 is a prayer written either about or by King Solomon—petitioning God to "Endow the King with your justice" (72:1), enable the king to "defend the afflicted among the people" (72:4), extend the reign of the king (72:5), use him to help the righteous flourish and to bring prosperity (72:6-7), receive tribute from other kings (72:9-10), deliver the needy (72:12), take pity on the weak (72:13), rescue the needy from oppressors and violence (72:14), and allow his name to endure forever (72:17). The Messianic king will prove to be a blessing to "all nations" (72:18). Thus, it is appropriate to pray for kings to rule according to the attributes of God, as well as to recognize that those who do will prove to be a blessing to people of different nations.

Within the Psalter, there is even a *genre* that is devoted to the themes of royalty, the Enthronement Psalms. One of the well-known Enthronement Psalms is Psalm 110. In it God is the conqueror who makes even his enemies submissive (v. 1), and he extends his "mighty scepter from Zion; [he] will rule in the midst of [his] enemies" (v. 2). He is depicted as maintaining "willing troops" (v. 3) and "arrayed in holy majesty." As a result, the Lord "will crush kings on the day of his wrath, he will judge the nations . . . and crush the rulers of the whole earth." (Ps. 110: 5-6). The Law of God is lauded (Ps. 19:7-12; Ps. 119) and is of universal application.

Never is the monarchical from of government condemned after its initiation, nor is a revolution called for to establish a democracy in its place. As foreign to modern governments as monarchy is, God does not deem this form as inherently evil. God's people are free to live and pursue their faith under the reign of a godly monarch or even under unbelievers, as long as other divine prerogatives are not trampled. Serving as monarch, David was never condemned by God for maintaining that role. However, prayers of imprecation against evil rulers (e.g. Ps. 7:6 ff.) indicate that not all monarchies are approved by God.

Proper Standards for Leaders (from Proverbs and Psalms)

Scripture is not silent on proper goals and conduct for leaders, addressing this area of ethics as few sources do. The prophets were keenly sensitive to the abuse of power by political leaders. The prophetical books warn rulers not to make unjust laws, issue oppressive decrees, deprive the poor of their rights, withhold justice, or rob the fatherless (Is. 10:1-2). Instead, they are to rule in conformity to Messiah's rule; they are to judge not by appearances (Is. 11:3) but by righteousness (Is. 11:4-5). An enduring ruler will be characterized by love for the people, faithfulness, justice, and righteousness (Is. 16:5). As early as Isaiah's time, it was recognized that "a king will reign in righteousness and rulers will rule with justice" (Is. 32:1).

The Messiah typifies the moral virtues necessary for leadership. He is characterized by justice, mercy, faithfulness (Is. 42:1-4), and "will not falter or be discouraged till he establishes justice on earth. In his law the islands will put their hope" (Is. 42:4). God's law and justice is to "become a light to the nations" (Is. 51:4), and the frequent command for rulers (and others) is: "Maintain justice and do what is right" (Is. 56:1). The royal leaders in Jeremiah's time were charged: "Administer justice every morning; rescue from the hand of his oppressor the one who has been robbed, or my wrath will break out and burn like fire" (Jer. 21:12). While evil kings were judged by God, the righteous king and his officials were to rescue the victim of robbery, treat the alien and fatherless fairly, not shed innocent blood, and obey the commands of God (Jer. 22:2-5). Public standards of righteousness were recognized throughout the OT. Citizens were not to defile their neighbor's wife, oppress the poor, rob, steal, or lend at an excessive interest rate (Ez. 18:11-13, 15-17).

Kings should serve as "foster fathers" and queens as "nursing mothers" (Is. 49:23). These comparisons to parental roles are as instructive, as they are inviolable. The nation, portrayed as a large extended family, is to be guided by leadership analogous to the tender, provident leadership of the home.

Kings were not secured by building great edifices, if they had employed the methods of unrighteousness and injustice (Jer. 22:13).

A king is not embellished by structural accomplishments (Jer. 22:15). God is not fooled by the external accomplishments of administrations. Instead of depending on physical achievements, the wise ruler will "defend the cause of the poor and needy" (Jer. 22:16) and avoid "dishonest gain, shedding innocent blood, and oppression and extortion" (Jer. 22:17). Kings rise and fall, and they are subject to the word of God (Jer. 1:10, 18-19).

The qualities of righteousness, justice, faithfulness, and mercy are frequently reiterated as desirable for political rulers. Governors are not required to be wealthy, strong, brilliant, attractive, nor famous; but these four virtues—righteousness, justice, faithfulness, and mercy—are essential.

Of course, the coming Messiah would perfectly fulfill all these attributes. He will bring peace such that "lambs and lions lie down together" (Is. 11:6), natural enemies would peacefully co-exist (Is. 11:9), and the "earth will be full of the knowledge of the Lord" (Is. 11:9). Messiah will cause many nations to marvel "and kings will shut their mouths because of him" (Is. 52:15). During his international reign there will be great peace, righteousness will be established: "Tyranny will be far from you . . . Terror will be far removed" (Is. 54:14). God's coming Messiah will be a righteous branch of David, "A king who will reign wisely and do what is just and right in the land" (Jer. 23:5).

Examples from Babylon in Daniel's time: Resistance, Deference, and Conviction

The Book of Daniel illustrates how believers must live under ungodly administrations. That the prophets were above any earthly administration and not obstructed from carrying out their proclamation is seen when the various prophets carried on their prophetic activity "during the reign of [various kings]" (Hos. 1:1; Am. 1:1; Mic. 1:1; Zeph. 1:1; and Zech. 1:1). Neither the form of government (monarchy), the quality of the particular ruler, nor the succession of power prevented the prophets from carrying out their ministry. The Word of the Lord is truly above temporal powers and is even addressed to the "royal house" (Hos. 5:1). Despite wicked administrations and their changes, Daniel was still able to maintain his integrity and serve the Lord.

The Book of Daniel touches on two very important matters: (1) how God works with unbelieving rulers, and (2) how the believer is to serve God above all others. Nebuchadnezzar's empire had developed to include prefects, governors, treasurers, judges, advisors, and assorted magistrates (Dan. 3:3). Moreover, his empire employed the Law of the Medes and Persians. The Medeo-Persian empire had codified that once the King issued a decree, the law was unalterable (Dan. 6:15). Desiring to avoid arbitrariness and flux, this policy advance could protect the people from arbitrary law that varied from ruler to ruler. It was also hoped that prior to instituting a final decree, this rule would force the ruler to consider consequences and aspects of the law, since it would become unalterable.

Daniel also tells the story of appropriate resistance to wrongful laws. Early on in the narrative, Daniel and his believing friends politely sought an exemption from a governmental decree. Daniel's polite but respectful entreaty should be understood as appropriate for a matter that was not a matter of conscience. Daniel asked to have a different diet, and in time demonstrated to the king the superior plan. Later, Daniel would interpret dreams for the king. After these episodes in which Daniel maintained his wisdom and integrity, the king elevated Daniel to be sub-Governor over the entire province (Dan. 4:48); he was also permitted to appoint his other believing friends to positions of leadership (4:49). Daniel's resistance in this case was different from subsequent cases.

Even though God was dealing with Nebuchadnezzar, he listened to bad advice. Some of Nebuchadnezzar's leaders conspired to have an unalterable decree issued, stipulating that any who did not worship an idol would be burned (Dan. 3:10-11). After Nebuchadnezzar consented, Daniel's friends protested and resisted. Still with respect, they stated the proper balance of priorities: "If we are thrown into the blazing furnace, the God we serve is able to save us from it, and he will rescue us from your hand, O king. But even if he does not, we want you to know, O king, that we will not serve your god or worship the image" (Dan. 3:17-18). God delivered the believers in this resistance, which led to Nebuchadnezzar's praise and decree: "Therefore I decree that the people of any nation or language who say anything against the God of Shadrach, Meshach, and Abednego be cut into pieces and their houses be turned into piles of rubble, for no other god can save in this way." (Dan. 3:29). The unbelieving king promoted the believers.

Nebuchadnezzar saw all this as God's sovereign hand. He publicly issued a decree, praising the God whose "kingdom is an eternal kingdom, his dominion endures from generation to generation" (Dan. 4:3). However, the next generation did not learn this enduring lesson, although Daniel endured.

King Darius, also tempted to deify the earthly ruler, approved a law that prayer should not be made to anyone except the king (Dan. 6:7). God delivered the resister again, and Daniel maintained respect, even wishing the king well when the miraculous deliverance was discovered (Dan. 6:21). Daniel was right in resisting a civil law that restricted his true faith and, in the end, King Darius learned the same lesson as Nebuchadnezzar before him had learned: God was superior to the king's law. He issued a decree that "in every part of my kingdom people must fear and reverence the God of Daniel" (Dan. 6:26). Darius came to see that the living God endured forever and "his kingdom will not be destroyed, his dominion will never end" (Dan. 6:26). God was Sovereign over sovereigns and resistance to impious laws was proper under certain conditions.

Other Pertinent Lessons

Cyrus was a strong king whose heart was moved by the Lord (Ez. 1:1). As a result, he issued an edict permitting the reconstruction of the Temple. Cyrus even contributed to the rebuilding by returning the articles which Nebuchadnezzar had appropriated (Ez. 1:7). During Ezra's time, following the exile, the Temple was rebuilt with private gifts, not state taxes (Ez. 2:69). The Emperor Cyrus actually protected God's people (Ez. 4:3, 5), an example of God using unbelieving rulers for good. Throughout his administration, there were numerous treasurers (Ez. 1:7), Governors and sub-governors (Ez. 6:6), censuses (Ez. 8:1-14; Neh. 7), and even royal archives (Ez. 6:6). The state apparatus included official correspondence from governmental leaders within the Bible, including actual letters from Darius, Xerxes, and others (Ez. 4:6; 5:7). The stable state had grown in its appreciation of precedent. By the time of Darius, the king realized the value of researching previous law to seek conformity to it (Ez. 5:17-6:3). Moreover, upon learning of previous legislation, Darius wisely supported it—even adding penalties to those who opposed the people of God (Ez. 6:11-12; cf. also Esther 1:19).

In Esther's time, the king issued an early edict of toleration, allowing the Jews the right to assemble, to protect themselves, to repel an attacking army, and to plunder their enemies (Esther 8:11). King Artaxerxes ordered that Ezra be given a subsidy to rebuild the Temple, lest the wrath of God break out in his empire; however, he prohibited Ezra from imposing taxes himself (Ez. 7:23-25). As Ezra and others see this, they praise God for the Sovereign Principle, for it is "the God of our fathers who has put it into the king's heart to bring honor to the house of the Lord in Jerusalem in this way" (Ez. 7:27). It was the Lord's doing through human rulers.

National confession was appropriate (Ez. 9:7), and Nehemiah served as a governor (Neh. 10:1). During Nehemiah's time, some early republican elements appear to be more institutionalized, as there were "leaders of the people,"(Neh. 10:17-27) and the citizens were led by lower level heads of family (Ez. 8:1; Neh. 7:5, 12:23). Monarchy is nowhere condemned, but God also uses grass-roots checks-and-balances and even unbelievers to accomplish his will. The Book of Esther illustrates respect for authority, patient dissent, and appropriate resistance to bad law. By the end of the OT, select governmental aspects had progressed significantly.

Cyrus, King of Persia, was a great ruler as well as fair to OT believers. One of the best summations of the final period of OT government is written by Plato who commends Cyrus as one of the fathers of good government.[64]

---

[64] Plato, *Laws* (New York: Penguin, 1970), 144.

Were the Greco-Roman Governments So Great? Plato and Aristotle

Between the close of the OT and the opening of the New Testament (hereafter, NT), two major types of development occurred that impact our study: philosophical and religious. Among the philosophical developments were the discourses of the Greeks (primarily Plato and Aristotle) and the Romans (e.g., Seneca and Cicero).

Plato's *Republic* is generally recognized as one of the earliest systematic treatises on the nature and form of government. In many ways it is a precursor to modern treatises on the state, complete with a humanistic orientation. In Book V of the *Republic*, Plato (428-387 BC) advocated ideas which are also associated with tyrannies: eugenics, genocide, class system—notions that were not subsequently copied except by the most inhumane governments. For Plato, the state was to be governed by guardians or philosopher-kings.[65] Guardians were to devote their entire lives to doing what was best for the country; conversely, they were to hold "the greatest repugnance to do what is against her interest." Such guardians were supposedly free from self-interest and to be trusted to protect the state's interest. This "higher class" would theoretically lead the state toward utopia.

Along with these seminal concepts were numerous notions that are recognized as fraught with error. The utopia envisioned in *The Republic* (Book III) was an early form of socialism,[66] as Plato advocated this ideal:

---

[65] "Neither cities nor States nor individuals will ever attain perfection until the small class of philosophers whom we termed useless but not corrupt are in consequence of some chance compelled . . . to undertake the care of the State, . . . or until kings, or if not kings, the sons of kings or princes, are divinely inspired with a true love of true philosophy." Ronald B. Levinson, ed., *A Plato Reader* (Boston: Houghton Mifflin Company, 1967), 273-274. Plato goes so far as to expect that, "the philosopher, holding converse with the divine order, becomes orderly and divine as far as the nature of man allows." Ibid., 275.

[66] To the embarrassment of humanists, this even extended to the sharing of wives and children in common in the perfect state. Levinson, op. cit., 310.

> In the first place, none of them [guardians] should have any property of his own beyond what is absolutely necessary; neither should they have a private house or store closed against anyone who has a mind to enter; their provisions should be only such as are required by trained warriors . . . And this will be their salvation, and they will be the *saviors* of the state. But should they ever acquire homes or lands or moneys of their own, they will become householders and husbandmen instead of guardians, enemies and tyrants instead of allies of the other citizens.[67]

The upward spiral of statist progress would advance from education.[68] Unaware of the effects of sin, Plato believed that, "the state, once started well, moves with accumulating force like a wheel. For where good nurture and education are maintained, they implant good constitutions, and these good constitutions taking root in a good education improve more and more, and this improvement affects the breed in man as in other animals."[69]

All of the presumed progress in the state was to lead to a utopian city, in which "all groups will call each other by such names as 'saviors' and 'helpers,' 'maintainers' and 'supporters' and that the guardians will call each other by family names such as 'brother' and 'son'; nor will these be empty words . . . This . . . will be a consequence also of the communal living and renunciation of property prescribed for the guardians. There will be no lawsuits among them arising from property or private family interests. Neither will there be suits for assault . . ."[70]

Justice, a central topic for the Greeks in pursuit of the improved city-state, was dependent on the rewards and results.[71] Its origin rested in mutual covenants as society progressed: "Justice arose when men discovered that being free to wrong others and being, in

---

[67] Ibid., 216. Emphasis added.

[68] Ibid., 222. "Education, I said, and nurture: if our citizens are well educated and grow into sensible men, they will easily see their way through . . ."

[69] Idem.

[70] Ibid., 248.

[71] Ibid., 187.

turn, liable to be wronged by others, was not in their interest; for only the few who were strong were able to benefit."[72]

Plato, like many other political theorists, believed in a certain evolution of the state. He identified five different types of government, the first (not needing a constitution) being monarchy or aristocracy, only varying as to whether it was one or a small number who ruled. This was followed by four other forms of government: the Spartan republican city-state ("which is generally applauded"), oligarchy ("which teems with evils"), democracy, and tyranny ("great and famous . . . worst disorder of a state"[73]). Plato suspected that an inevitability was attached to these such that, unless led by Platonic guardians of the Republic, the state would naturally deteriorate in stages from monarchy to democracy and ultimately devolve to tyranny. Not only does this notion seem incompatible with his earlier optimism about the nature of man, but these five forms of government are also paired with five psychological dispositions of various personality types.

The evolution of the state commenced with family rule. At first, elders who "by virtue of having inherited power from his father and mother" ruled; shortly thereafter, came patriarchy, followed by rule of mini-monarchs. After that came the next necessary step that was "to choose some representatives to review the rules of all the families, and to propose openly to the leaders and heads of the people—the 'kings,' so to speak—the adoption of those rules that particularly recommend themselves for common use. These representatives will be known as lawgivers, and by appointing the leaders as officials, they will create out of the separate autocracies a sort of aristocracy, or perhaps kingship. And while the political system passes through the transitional state, they will administer the state themselves."[74] From there, due to excess of liberty, states devolve to democracies, then to anarchies.

Plato acknowledged two fundamental types of constitutional government: monarchy (which was taken to extremes by the

---

[72] Ibid., 187.

[73] Ibid., 311.

[74] Plato, *Laws* (New York: Penguin, 1970), 125.

Persians) and democracy (embodied by Athens) which was corrupted by excessive liberty.[75] He argued, "It is absolutely vital for a political system to combine them, if it is to enjoy freedom and friendship allied with good judgment."[76] Plato ranked the various governmental options for beginning a society: "The ideal starting point is dictatorship [benevolent], the next best is constitutional kingship, and the third is some sort of democracy. Oligarchy comes fourth . . ."[77]

His favored model was a timocracy (the rule of honor), in which the philosopher-guardians would rule according to a constitution. However, if the education described above was not successful, the government would degenerate into the next most preferable form of government, an oligarchy (rule of the few). This rule of the few comes about when the ambition and rivalry of others motivates them to seek power. Upon the heels of oligarchy comes a democracy, "a charming form of government, full of variety and disorder, and dispensing a sort of equality to equals and unequals alike."[78]

Democracy (associated with "drones") is not a superior form of government; rather, one which is dominated by appetite, greed, and immoderation. In the transition from oligarchy to democracy, citizens confuse insolence with breeding, and term "anarchy liberty, waste magnificence, and impudence courage."[79] It results in "libertinism of useless and unnecessary pleasures."

This excessive increase in liberty produces a negative and doleful reaction, which leads to tyranny. Concludes Plato: "The excess of liberty, whether in states or individuals, seems only to pass into excess slavery. And so it is from democracy, and from no other source, that tyranny naturally arises, and the harshest and most

---

[75] Of Athens, Plato commented that, "complete freedom from all authority is infinitely worse than submitting to a moderate degree of control." Plato, *Laws* (New York: Penguin, 1970), 150.

[76] Plato, *Laws* (New York: Penguin, 1970), 144.

[77] Ibid., 167.

[78] Ronald B. Levinson, ed., *A Plato Reader* (Boston: Houghton Mifflin Company, 1967), 324.

[79] Ibid., 327.

complete form of tyranny and slavery out of the most extreme form of liberty."[80]

This downward spiral among constitutional forms of government (from enlightened republic to oligarchy to democracy and finally to tyranny) is inevitable without the elite republican guardians. Optimistically based on human enlightenment, Plato exhibited an approach to government that was later revived by modern theorists. However, it also bore within its bosom seeds of inhumane ideas, such as socialism, elitism, and class-inevitability. Progressive though these ideas were for their time, they were still inferior to the political wisdom manifested in Scripture.

In Plato's *Laws*,[81] he also championed a structured state with a communist basis. Written in the mid-fourth century BC as Plato's final political sermon, the *Laws* sets forth the necessity of laws as a balance to the absence of the ideal ruler. Far more realistic (and we would say informed by depravity), this final political work by Plato sets forth the protections necessary for the state that does not have a benevolent dictator.

Plato goes so far as to describe concretely his utopia, Magnesia. He believed that this planned state will be based on unchanging moral absolutes that are embodied in the law code.[82] The location was to be 9-10 miles from the sea and populated by 5,040 citizens, mostly farmers. Education plays a primary role in this utopia, promising to produce excellent citizens.

Even though not known for his religious devotion, at the outset of his consideration of constitutions, Plato said, "Let us therefore summon God to attend the foundation of the state. May he hear our prayers, and having heard, come graciously and benevolently to help us settle our state and its laws."[83] Shortly thereafter, Plato seems to

---

[80] Ibid., 330.

[81] Plato also wrote *Politicus* (or The Statesman), a practical manual for the statesman. Trevor Saunders views this as a "bridge between the *Republic* and the *Laws*." Plato, *Laws* (New York: Penguin, 1970), 25. His view is that the *Republic* sets forth the ideal, with the *Laws* setting forth constitutional realities. In between is the *via media* of *Politicus*.

[82] Plato, *Laws* (New York: Penguin, 1970), 29.

[83] Ibid., 169.

advocate a theocracy, or more accurately a polytheocracy: "But if that's the sort of principle on which your new state is to be named, it should be called after the god who really does rule over men who are rational enough to let him."[84] He also noted that, "Justice . . . takes vengeance on those who abandon the divine law. . . . So what conduct recommends itself to God and reflects his wishes? There is only one sort . . . In our view it is God who is pre-eminently the 'measure of all things,'. . . on this principle the moderate man is God's friend."[85] Plato also expected religious leaders to play a prominent public role: "Temples should be built round the marketplace and on high ground round the perimeter . . . Next to them should be administrative offices and courts of law. This is holy ground, and here–partly because the legal cases involve solemn religious issues, partly because of the august divinities whose temples are nearby—judgment will be given and sentence received."[86]

From a modern vantage point, or from the scriptural tradition, one may easily note ideas advocated by Plato that exhibit serious deficiencies. The following expressions endorsed by Plato, should definitely be questioned before being implemented.

* Plato advocated the following as an exemplary (we would say intrusive) law: "A man must marry between the ages of thirty and thirty-five. If he does not, he must be punished by fines and disgrace."[87]
* Citizens would be selected based on their ability. Plato even speaks of a purge, sounding eerily like ethnic cleansing. Like a shepherd who "will weed out the unhealthy and inferior stock and send it off to other herds, and keep only the thoroughbreds and the healthy animals . . . it is vitally important for the legislator to ascertain and explain the appropriate measures in each case, not only as regards a purge, but in general. To purge a whole state, for instance, several methods may be employed,

---

[84] Ibid., 170.
[85] Ibid., 174.
[86] Ibid., 259.
[87] Ibid., 183.

some mild, some drastic; and if a legislator were a dictator too he'd be able to purge the state drastically, which is the best way."[88]

* Strict distribution of property, with little personal ownership: "So what's the correct method of distribution? First, one has to determine what the total number of people ought to be, then agree on the question of the distribution of the citizens and decide the number and size of the subsection into which they ought to be divided; and the land and houses must be divided equally among these subsections."[89]

* Coercive communism is endorsed: "'Friends' property is genuinely shared'[90] is put into practice as widely as possible throughout the entire state. Now I don't know whether in fact this situation—a community of wives, children and all property—exists anywhere today, or will ever exist, but at any rate in such a state the notion of private property will have been by hook or by crook completely eliminated from life. Everything possible will have been done to throw into a sort of common pool even what is by nature 'my own.'"[91]

* Moreover, hard currency for savings would be illegal: "No private person shall be allowed to possess any gold or silver, but only coinage for day-to-day dealings . . . If a private individual should ever need to go abroad, he should first obtain leave of the authorities, and if he returns home with some surplus foreign money in his pocket he must deposit it with the state and take local money to the same value in exchange. If he is found keeping it for himself, it must be confiscated by the state. If anyone who knows of its concealment fails to report it, he must be liable to a curse and a reproach, and in addition be fined in a sum not less than that of the foreign currency brought in."[92]

---

[88] Ibid., 202.

[89] Ibid., 205.

[90] Ernest Barker notes that Pythagoras anticipated Plato with the principle of *koina ta ton philon* (The goods of friends are common property.). Ernest Barker, *The Political Thought of Plato and Aristotle* (New York: Dover, 1959), 21.

[91] Plato, *Laws* (New York: Penguin, 1970), 207-208.

[92] Ibid., 211.

* Women are looked down on as inferior in virtue to men and resistant to communal equality: "Women have got used to a life of obscurity and retirement, and any attempt to force them into the open will provoke tremendous resistance from them, and they'll be more than a match for the legislator."[93]

* Perhaps most illustrative of the danger of over-legislating are Plato's laws attempting to regulate procreation, as a way of having the family "present the state with the best and finest children they can produce. . . . but if they act carelessly, or are incapable of intelligent action . . . the results are deplorable."[94] If the family is obligated to the state,[95] then laws regulating procreation are needed. Plato advocated invasiveness to the extent below:

> So the bridegroom had better . . . approach the task of begetting children with a sense of responsibility, and the bride should do the same, especially during the period when no children have yet been born to them. They should be supervised by women whom we have chosen . . . These women must assemble daily at the temple . . . for not more than a third of the day, and when they have convened each must report to her colleagues any wife or husband of childbearing age she has seen who is concerned with anything but the duties imposed on him or her . . . If children come in suitable numbers, the period of supervised procreation should be ten years and no longer. But if a couple remain childless throughout this period, they should part, and call in their relatives and the female officials to help them decide terms of divorce . . . If some dispute arises about the duties and interests of the parties, they must choose ten of the Guardians of the Laws [to arbitrate] . . . The female officials must enter the homes of the young people and by combination of admonition and threats try to make them give up their ignorant and sinful ways.[96]

---

[93] Ibid., 263.

[94] Ibid., 267.

[95] Ernest Barker characterizes Plato's elevation of the state over the family: "They [homes] shelter at best a restricted family feeling; they harbor at the worst avarice and ignorance. Pull down the walls, and let the free air of a common life blow over the place where they have been." Ernest Barker, op. cit., 143.

[96] Plato, *Laws* (New York: Penguin, 1970), 267.

If such police-state tactics did not work, then higher authorities were to intervene. The law continued: "Unless the person whose name is posted up succeeds in convicting in court those who published the notice, he must be deprived of the privilege of attending weddings and parties celebrating the birth of children. If he persists in attending, anyone who wishes should chastise him by beating him, and not be punished for it."[97] Likewise, adultery was regulated, not so much for morality or the individuals but for the interests of the state: "When children have been produced as demanded by law, if a man has intercourse with another woman, or a woman with another man, and the other party is still of an age to bear children, they must suffer the same penalty as was specified for those who are still having children."[98]

The above show the excess of statist legislation at a very early date. The state-intrusive form of government leads to similar abuses to the government of the family as well as to the responsibility of the individual.

Many champion the supposed excellencies of Platonic government. For example, Ernest Barker lauds: "A sense of the value of the individual was thus the primary condition of the development of political thought in Greece. . . . in Greece, as contrasted with the rest of the ancient world, man was less sacrificed to the whole . . . each man counted for what he was worth . . . Here were individuals distinct from the state."[99] Many others extol the humanistically-viewed virtues of Greek politics.

However, as one reviews the archaic, often-authoritative, and communistic notions in Plato's writings, one wonders if the politics of Plato are improvements over the republic of Moses after all. It seems that its laudable aspects are repetitions of the best of OT government, while its deficiencies diminish it considerably below the level of divinely revealed government. One might be wise to

---

[97] Ibid., 268.

[98] Ibid.

[99] Ernest Barker, *The Political Thought of Plato and Aristotle* (New York: Dover, 1959), 2-3.

question if the earliest Greek philosophers were superior to the wisdom of God.

Aristotle

Later, Aristotle (384-322 BC) would further enhance the maturing views of good government. Both critical of and superior to Plato, Aristotle set forth a very detailed and sophisticated set of political considerations. Aristotle treated ethics as a branch of politics, viewing politics as "the supreme practical science to which all others are subordinate."[100] Aristotle's best guide for political virtue, however, was no higher than the pleasure or pain related to political decisions. Moral virtues, therefore, were the means between extremes. This Aristotelian moderation and calculation, regardless of its other deficiencies, did lead to an advance in categorization. Aristotle recognized justice as either that which was lawful or as that which was fair and equal. Aristotle's notion of justice was not exclusively governmental, as he also referred to the exchange of goods from farmers or manufacturers as instances of justice.[101] Justice was further defined as "equality for equals, inequality for unequals"[102]—an improvement over Plato.

Aristotle also had a more realistic view of the utility of private property. Likely with Plato in mind, Aristotle argued: "None of these advantages is secured by those who seek excessive unification of the state. And what is more, they are openly throwing away the practice of two virtues—self-restraint with regard to women and liberality with regard to property. The abolition of private property will mean that no man will be seen to be liberal and no man will ever do any act of liberality; for it is in the use of articles that liberality is practiced."[103] The amount of pleasure received from the ownership of private property was not wrong as long as it was not excessive. Within moderation, the ownership of private property

---

[100] Sir David Ross, *Aristotle* (London: Muthuen & Co, Ltd, 1971), 187.

[101] Ibid., 213.

[102] Ibid., 253.

[103] Aristotle, *The Politics* (New York: Penguin, 1992), 115.

may even bring pleasure and allow for charitably caring for one's neighbor.

Although Alexander the Great, the Empire builder, identified himself as a pupil of Aristotle, nevertheless, Aristotle thought in terms of city government, not imperial polity. Aristotle thought that city-governance was perhaps the highest form possible—"any larger aggregate was . . . a mere tribe or ill-knit congeries of people."[104] The political unit grew from the minimum society (the family) to the village to the city. It must be realized that for Aristotle matters of the state *per se* were technically beyond the scope of much of his discussion in *Politica*, in that Aristotle restricted his treatise primarily to an intermediate level of governance. Slavery was accepted as a fact of political life in his time (*Politica* I, 3-7). Aristotle condoned: "That one should command and another obey is both necessary and expedient. Indeed some things are so divided right from birth, some to rule, some to be ruled."[105] Moreover, Aristotle was not a champion of egalitarianism: "For the male is more fitted to rule than the female, unless conditions are quite contrary to nature."[106]

One of the contributions of Aristotle to western political thought was his classification of various forms of government. Having studied 158 various Greek constitutions—evidence that the idea of constitutions is not a product of the Enlightenment or any other modern contrivance—Aristotle was able to set forth a political taxonomy. He conceived of three proper forms: monarchy, aristocracy, and constitutional republic. Each of these legitimate forms also had a mirror-imaged deviation, respectively: tyranny, oligarchy, and democracy.[107] Each of these deviations would take a legitimate variable and extend it beyond moderation. Monarchy identified order as the supreme virtue; aristocracy saw class as the supreme virtue; republicanism saw moderation as virtue; democracy viewed free birth as its highest principle; oligarchy thought of

---

[104] Sir David Ross, *Aristotle* (London: Muthuen & Co, Ltd, 1971), 237.

[105] Aristotle, *The Politics* (New York: Penguin, 1992), 67.

[106] Ibid., 92.

[107] Sir David Ross, *Aristotle* (London: Muthuen & Co, Ltd, 1971), 250.

wealth as its major virtue; and a tyranny justified itself in terms of the principle of force. Corruptions or deviations arose when the subsidiary aims were confused with the supreme virtue. Plato had similarly categorized the various options of governmental form.

At various times, Aristotle argued for the necessity of the involvement of the many. He feared a monarchy without the mediating influence of the many. Aristotle proffered four reasons for the many to have a voice in government: (1) sounding like Solomon before him, Aristotle believed that many ordinary people acting collectively would normally be better than a few; (2) the indefinite exclusion of citizens from decisions effecting them builds discontent; (3) elections in themselves have benefit; and (4) "[t]he individual is likely to be overcome by passion; a multitude are unlikely all to get into a passion at once."[108] Still however, he preferred a modified monarchy, one with a leader like a president or a prime minister.

Aristotle ranked the forms of government as follows: (1) monarchy, (2) an aristocracy of benevolent rulers, or (3) a constitutional republic; next, (4) democracies and (5) oligarchies were preferred over (6) tyrannies. In sum, he was convinced that the better forms of government allowed the best men to rule, all the while subject to some scheme of check-and-balance. He was also sophisticated enough to have identified an evolutionary tendency among all governmental forms. Aristotle noted that monarchies tended to evolve into aristocracies and oligarchies, while tyrannies tended to evolve toward democracies; and democracies tended to mutate from the most moderate toward the least moderate. A political version of the Law of Entropy provided Aristotle with leverage to warn against such dangerous tendencies. To the modern reader, Aristotle indeed seems to speak in familiar tones.

Aristotle was prescient to advise: "Without the moral end a state becomes a mere alliance, and law a mere convention and security against injustice without any positive power to make men good."[109] For all these advances and even with the clarity of thought,

---

108 Ibid., 254.
109 Ibid., 253.

nonetheless, Aristotle fell very short of the biblical views of government. Indeed, a case can be made that most of his contributions were imitations of either Scripture or biblical truths viewed retrospectively through the rise and fall of nations.

The Theology of Freedom: From the Greeks or the Bible?

Christianity, rather than Greek thought, ushered in significant alterations of her own in matters of state. Although many modern democracies blur the issues (and the attendant world views), distinctive and major differences can be seen between pre-Christian and post-Christian politics. Christianity brought with it not only change to the individual soul but also change to the *polis*. The democratic and republican impulses that would become associated with Christianity were indeed spawned by biblical fidelity, not by some of the pre-Christian philosophies. Frequently, assertions are made that ancient Greece with its city-states and Rome with its Senate are the true precursors of modern democracies. A stronger case, however, can be made to the contrary, that modern democracies are more beholden to revealed religion than to Greco-Roman innovations in government.

Evans claims, "In ancient Greece and Rome . . . one set of assumptions prevailed concerning religious questions, and a particular kind of politics was developed; in Judeo-Christian culture, a totally different set of axioms appeared, and the political/economic outcomes were changed as well."[110]

Furthermore, he argues that human freedom is better supported by the biblical worldview than by the Greco-Roman paradigm. He rightly notes that theological premises lead to numerous ideological clashes over matters of statecraft, the nature of society, the significance of the individual, and the power of political officials. The contrarian contends: "In the conventional history lesson, paganism is identified with the cause of liberty, Christianity with oppression. We are used to hearing much about Periclean Athens or

---

[110] M. Stanton Evans, *The Theme is Liberty: Religion, Politics, and the American Tradition* (Washington, DC: Regnery, 1994), 118-119.

Republican Rome, the thought of Plato and Aristotle, and so on, as if these were the ancestors of our freedom. Concerning all the major points at issue, such teachings are woefully mistaken."[111]

Evans goes so far as to claim: "The critical proposition is as follows: *The ancients knew nothing of our ideas of limited government and personal liberty, and given their peculiar conception of the world could not have done so.*"[112] Although Aristotle is often cited as exemplary of the pinnacle of pre-Christian political thought and "often cited as a precursor of our institutions," Evans asserts, nevertheless, "But so far as human freedom is concerned, Aristotle is about as far from our beliefs as it is possible to get." Evans notes that Aristotle is "hardly a spokesman for personal freedom or limited government, and could not conceivably be the source of our ideas about these subjects. Had we quoted instead the works of Plato—well known for their authoritarianism—the point would be even more explicit."

Religious Parties at the Time of Christ

Between the testaments, at least four Jewish political groups arose: (1) Pharisees, (2) Sadducees, (3) Essenes, and (4) Zealots. The Pharisees first appeared during the Hasmonean era and sought to control the religion of the state. They argued that the disobedience of Israel led to the Babylonian Captivity (a manifest example of God's judgment on a nation) and asserted strict adherence to the Mosaic Law as a national remedy. The Sadducees were a more aristocratic group, who may have originally been high-ranking fiscal officers. More open to Greek influences, the Sadducees did not have the constant adversarial relationship with the Romans that the Pharisees and Zealots did. The Essene community at Qumran evolved in the second century BC and offered an ascetic lifestyle, complete with property held in common.[113] This early socialism was

---

[111] Ibid., 132.

[112] Ibid., 132-133.

[113] Raymond F. Surburg, *Introduction to the Intertestamental Period* (St. Louis: Concordia Publishing House, 1975), 58.

likely more religious in origin than in imitation of Plato's ideal. In the Essenes' *Manual of Discipline for the Future Congregation of Israel*, a concise religious constitution is given. It required the frequent reading of the law and the provisions of the covenant with male participation at incremental levels.[114] The Zealots were an activist group founded in AD 6 after the revolt of Judas the Galilean. These tax protesters opposed paying taxes to foreign powers, considering such an act of treason against Israel's true and only King.

Oscar Cullmann asserted that several of Jesus' disciples were associated with the Zealot party,[115] while Jesus was crucified for a crime associated with the Zealot political party.[116] Cullmann also noted that, while the options were pressed on him, Jesus refused to endorse either the Sadducee-collaborationist option, or the Zealot-revolutionist option. Cullmann believed that Jesus maintained a finely circumscribed position: "On the one hand, the state is nothing final. On the other, it had the right to demand what is necessary to its existence—but no more. Every totalitarian claim of the state is thereby disallowed. And the double imperative logically follows: on the one hand, do not let the Zealots draw you into a purely political martial action against the existence of the Roman State; on the other, do not give to the state what belongs to God! . . . if ever the state demands what belongs to God, if ever it hinders you in the proclamation of the Kingdom of God, then resist it."[117] According to Cullmann, Jesus maintained a critical, albeit permissive, attitude toward the state—not deeming it a "final institution."[118] Cullmann's

---

[114] Theodor H. Gaster, *The Dead Sea Scriptures* (New York: Anchor, 1976), 438-440. At 20, the young man could have probationary status and give legal testimony. At 25, he took full citizenship in the community and may hold office. At 30, he may judge and take part in litigation. Heads of families were still in existence, and the Manual provides other institutional guidance, despite its brevity.

[115] Oscar Cullmann, *The State in the New Testament* (New York: Charles Scribner's Sons, 1956), 17. He suggested Simon (Mt. 10:4), Judas (Jn. 6:71), or possibly even Peter.

[116] Ibid., 12, 42-49.

[117] Ibid., 37.

[118] Ibid., 19.

formulation was: "On the one hand, we see that he certainly does not regard the state as in any sense a *final*, divine institution; on the other hand, we see that he accepts the state and radically renounces every attempt to overthrow it."[119]

The key lesson from this survey is that as the New Testament opens a rather sophisticated range of governmental theories and options were already known. Moreover, Jesus could have chosen to endorse or oppose any of those. As one searches the Gospels, therefore, he will look to see if Jesus opposes, supports, modifies, or transforms pre-existing concepts.

Below is a summary of OT Foundations from this chapter in answer to its major question:

(1) God revealed a republican form of government to Moses.
(2) Decentralized office-holders and judges are seen before Israel's monarchy.
(3) Political wisdom warned against the dangers of a centralized monarchy.
(4) The revealed Psalms and Proverbs provide abiding lessons in governance.
(5) There is a place for resistance to tyranny.
(6) God warned against entangling alliances, but he still uses unbelieving rulers.
(7) The secular governments before the time of Christ were far from perfect; and should be called into question rather than slavishly imitated.

Quite a bit of political information is given for many political structures, for day-to-day governance, and for guidance in all centuries. Short of some form of extremely biased prejudice or a commitment to limit information, is there any sound reason *not* to allow the Bible to speak to matters of governance, especially when it can offer enhancements, support of liberty, or civic stability?

---

[119] Ibid., 18. Cullmann is also quick to note that although this attitude has aspects of tension in it, it is not contradictory.

Chapter 3

Christians and Politics Today: Any Sources of Wisdom?

In view of the question that concludes the previous chapter, then, let us grow more specific and ask: What sources might be helpful to deal with modern questions? Does a person or a believer necessarily have to reject all religious teaching or can valid revealed ideas call into question modern politics? If so, are there specific verses or information that can guide us?

Some Christians are prone, usually after they have been battered a bit by secular experts, to say: "The Bible says nothing about politics. There's not a shred of guidance for modern political issues." Besides being a premature concession, this faulty view has at least three major problems with it. *First*, to maintain that view practically requires one to shrink the canon of Scripture and ignore or explain away the many verses with political wisdom. *Second*, that minimization of biblical content does not fit with the history of biblical exegesis; there are actually numerous volumes, sermons, commentaries, and treatises from Christians in prior generations who set forth valid and insightful biblical instruction from *sola scriptura*. *Third*, the view that the Bible does not speak to political questions renders Christianity as either gnostic or unhelpful in a key area of life.

Instead of this premature surrender, it seems preferable to question many of the political givens of our day to see how they fare in light of transcultural scripture. Surely, all but the most extreme would grant that Christ revealed information about governance.

Gospel Politics: The Teachings of Christ on Matters of State

The magisterial teachings on matters of state have a *prima facie* preference insofar as they are the most direct sayings of Christ on these subjects. Christians of all traditions affirm their commitment to the pre-eminence of Christ (Col. 1:18) in all things—certainly not excluding the political realm. Thus, there is a natural tendency to elevate the actual words of Christ over other parts of revelation. While this sensitivity is needed, one also desires to interpret Christ's teachings consistently with other revelation. In light of the relatively small amount of Christ's express teachings on matters of state, his words should not be depicted to discount other scriptural teachings; rather, his teaching is in harmony with other parts of revelation (2 Tim. 3:16).

It is important, of course, to note from the outset that Jesus did not present himself as a worldly political leader. He could have chosen that role, had he desired, but he did not. He came as Messiah, and that Messianic role included other offices (such as prophet, priest, and king; cf. *Westminster Shorter Catechism* #23). A key distinction arises in the early pages of the gospel narratives: Jesus accepts the attributions of a monarch, but he is not a king of a visible, geographical kingdom.

Jesus as King: And there can be more than one king at a time

Early in the Advent narratives, Jesus' kingship is revealed. When the magi searched for him, they asked "for the one who has been born king of the Jews" (Mt. 2:2). Clearly, they perceived Jesus to be a king in keeping with the prophecy of Micah that out of Judah would come "a ruler who will be the shepherd of my people" (Mic. 5:2; Mt. 2:6). Many other passages refer to Jesus as a king. Toward the end of his life, he told his disciples that "at the renewal of all things" he would sit on a glorious throne, along with the disciples (Mt. 19:28). That this royal prerogative was clearly understood may be seen when Zebedee's wife asks permission for her two sons to sit on the right and the left "in your kingdom" (Mt. 20:21). As Jesus entered Jerusalem on Palm Sunday, he was greeted as the coming king of David (Mk. 11:10) and as the king who comes in fulfillment of Zechariah's prophecy (Zech. 9:9; Mt. 21:5). His kingship was so imminent that he taught, "I tell you the truth, some who are standing here will not taste death before they see the kingdom of God come with power" (Mk. 9:1), indicating that his kingship was not solely eschatological.

As Jesus instituted the Lord's Supper, he prophesied that a day would come when he shared the fruit of the vine with the disciples "in my Father's kingdom" (Mt. 26:29). To have been emphasized on that occasion, obviously, the sovereign rule of Christ with the Father was a prominent teaching. Various rulers investigating the charges against Jesus witnessed his claims to kingship. When Pilate asked Jesus, "Are you the king of the Jews?", he answered in the affirmative (Mk. 15:2; Mt. 27:11). Pilate presented Jesus to the accusing crowd as "your king" (Jn. 19:14-15), to which the people responded by pledging loyalty only to Caesar—certainly a case of historic hypocrisy. When Jesus was hanged on the cross, the soldiers placed a mock crown of thorns on his head and cry, "Hail, king of the Jews" (Mt. 27:29). As Jesus was on the cross, his tormentors posted a sign (in three languages) with political import: This is Jesus, the King of the Jews (Mt. 27:37; Jn. 19:19). The Jews were quick to dispute this, begging for the sign to state merely that Jesus "claimed" to be a king (Jn. 19:21).

However, Jesus clarified what kind of king he was on several occasions. As Christ was arrested in Gethsemane, Peter cut off the ear of one of Jesus' captors. Jesus ordered Peter to re-sheath his sword because the disciples were not to oppose this arrest, as it was part of the sovereign will of God (Mt. 26:54). Jesus instructed his disciples not to oppose this arrest because had he desired he could have called on his Father who would "at once put at my disposal more than twelve legions of angels" (Mt. 26:53). In this verse, he revealed that earthly political developments are subject to the divine plan, regardless of how perilous they appear. For the Christian, there can be no more critical moment than this when the Lord's fate was at stake. Yet, rather than calling disciples to fight with the weapons of this world (2 Cor. 10:4-5), Jesus taught that a categorically different and superior monarchical plan is at work. He never tried to assert himself as a worldly ruler.

In John 18, Jesus was investigated by the Roman Governor, Pilate, who asked him directly, "Are you the king of the Jews?" (Jn. 18: 33). Jesus wanted to know if the query was based on others' opinions or Pilate's own (Jn. 18:34), and then answered, "My kingdom is not of this world. If it were, my servants would fight to prevent my arrest by the Jews. But now my kingdom is from another place" (Jn. 18:36). Jesus explicitly affirmed that neither his kingdom nor its source was of this world. It was from a transcendent locale, and not to be confused with the fickle dynasties of this world. When further pressed by Pilate, Jesus again averred that he was correct in noting that "I am a king. In fact for this very reason I was born and for this I came into the world to testify to the truth" (Jn. 18:37). Hence, Jesus himself taught clearly and often his own kingship, which was over a kingdom that was "within" (Lk. 17:21). He explicitly denied that it was visible or detectable by careful observation (Lk. 17:20-21).

His kingship is seen by two other clear proofs. *First*, he announces the arrival of the kingdom of God. He called on his listeners to repent, for the kingdom of heaven was near (Mt. 4:17); he blessed the impoverished of spirit as the heirs to the kingdom of heaven (Mt. 5:3); he prayed for the kingdom of God to come to earth as it was already operating in heaven (Mt. 6:10); the disciples are charged to preach the nearness of the kingdom of heaven (Mt. 10:7); and since John the Baptist's time, "the kingdom of heaven has been forcefully advancing" (Mt. 11:12). In addition, followers of Christ will take their place at a great feast "in the kingdom of heaven" (Mt. 8:11), while unbelievers are called "subjects of the kingdom" (Mt. 8:12).

Second, in many of the parables Jesus directly and unavoidably ties himself to the kingdom motif when he invoked, "The kingdom of heaven is like . . ." (Mt. 13:19, 24, 31, 44, 47; 20:21; 22:2; 25:1; Mk. 4:26, 30). Many of the parables serve to illustrate kingdom truths, an indication that the governmental dimension is not denied by Jesus.

On no occasion did Jesus repudiate the title of king or deny its governmental aspects. Yet, he was careful to distinguish his kingship from the human political administrations of his day. A later statement of faith describes the kingship of Jesus in these terms: "Christ executes the office of a king, in calling out of the world a people to himself, and giving them officers, laws, and censures by which he visibly governs them; in bestowing saving grace upon his elect, rewarding their obedience, and correcting them for their sins, preserving and supporting then under all their temptations and sufferings, restraining and overcoming all their enemies, and powerfully ordering all things for his own glory, and their good; and also taking vengeance on the rest who know not God and obey not the gospel."[120] On the kingship of Christ, Carl Henry comments:

> Jesus in his own person is the embodied sovereignty of God. He lives out that sovereignty in the flesh. He manifests the kingdom of God by enthroning the creation-will of God and demonstrating his lordship over Satan. Jesus conducts himself as Lord and true King, ruling over human hearts, ruling over demons, ruling over nature at its fiercest, ruling over sickness, conquering death itself. With the coming of Jesus the kingdom is not merely immanent; it gains the

---

[120] *Westminster Larger Catechism,* Question #45.

larger scope of incursion and invasion. . . . He reveals God's royal power in its salvific activity.[121]

Basic Governmental Prerogatives Accepted by Jesus

Jesus had several occasions to encourage the overthrow of certain governmental prerogatives. It is interesting to note two major areas where Jesus did not overthrow the existing government: the use of the military and taxation.

Several military figures appear in the Gospels. In Matthew 8, a centurion asked Jesus to heal his servant (Mt. 8:5). After the healing was completed, rather than rebuking this centurion for service in the military and calling for him to resign his commission, Jesus commended him: "I tell you the truth, I have not found anyone in Israel with such great faith" (Mt. 8:10; cf. Lk. 7:1-10 for a fuller account). A "royal official" also requested healing for his son (Jn. 4:49, 53). At the crucifixion of Jesus, one centurion believes and confesses Christ (Lk. 23:47). Elsewhere in the NT, others served in the military with no moral disapprobation. The Book of Acts speaks of Cornelius as a god-fearing centurion (Acts 10:1-2).

The primary concern of Jesus is not to call disciples out of the military, but to call them to moral and righteous living within that profession. John the Baptist gave inquiring soldiers these instructions: "Don't extort money and don't accuse people falsely; be content with your pay" (Lk. 3:14). Neither does John treat military service as an inherently corrupt vocation. There were also, of course, unethical military police (Mt. 27:11-14). Contrary to some theories, Jesus did not oppose the military *per se*; he only sought to govern it according to divine morality.

Contrary to the pacifist illusion, Jesus explicitly repudiated that he had come to bring peace (Mt. 10:34; Lk. 12:51); rather, "a sword"—the symbol for civil or military force. Luke recorded Jesus as saying, "Do you think I came to bring peace on earth? No, I tell you, but division" (Lk. 12:51).

---

[121] Carl F. H. Henry, "Reflections on the Kingdom of God," *Journal of the Evangelical Theological Society*, vol., 35, no. 1 (March 1992), 42.

Jesus even spoke of military tactics in a parable about two warring kings. Jesus was aware of and did not condemn the use of military intelligence to "consider whether he is able with ten thousand men to oppose the one coming against him with 20,000" (Lk. 14:31). If the king cannot reasonably win that battle, then he will sue for peace (Lk. 14:32). None of this is overturned by Jesus the Realist.

Tax collection was also legal, as can be seen from numerous passages (Mk. 2:14-17; Mt. 5:46; Mt. 9:9-12; Mt. 21:31-32; Lk. 3:12-13). Jesus called one tax collector to be a disciple (Mk. 2:14), and did not let his profession prevent him from dining with him. Repentant tax-collectors could enter heaven sooner than unrepentant Pharisees (Lk. 18:13-14). Similar to military professionals, tax collectors were not told to abandon their profession but to serve ethically in it (Lk. 3:12-13). In Luke 19:1-10, Zaccheus was converted and served as a prime example of ethical tax-collection and restitution. Taxation was apparently acceptable to Jesus. In the Book of Acts, the first convert from Africa was an Ethiopian official who was involved in the treasury of Queen Candace (Acts 8:37). Thus, by inference, governments are permitted to tax and they may organize for the efficient collection and preservation of those revenues.

Jesus is clear on the propriety of taxation. Jesus' parents trek to his birth-site as part of a taxation and census that is not condemned after the fact (Lk. 2:1-2). On several occasions, Jesus had opportunity to encourage his disciples to refrain from paying taxes, but he consistently refused. Matthew 17:24-27 contains the episode of paying the temple tax. Jesus' support of taxation is enhanced when it is noted that this was a religious tax. Not only did he advocate the paying of civil taxes, but politico-religious taxes as well. The tax collectors from the Capernaum Temple asked Peter if his teacher paid the "temple tax." (Mt. 17:24). Evidently, there were some who did not customarily pay this. Peter defended Jesus as complying. Later, when discussing this matter, Jesus made two salient points for all disciples.

First, he warned them that tax collectors tend to favor certain groups ("their own sons"—Mt. 17:25), while seeking higher payment from other groups. This inequity is clearly not condoned by Jesus. Noting that most taxes in biblical times were either fixed in terms of amount (Mt. 17:24) or fixed in terms of percentages (not graduated as in some modern systems), still it must be reckoned that the government is permitted to set the ranges of taxation. *Second*, Jesus taught that the payment of taxes should be continued "so that we may not offend them" (Mt. 17:27). He then instructed Peter to open the mouth of the first fish he caught and pay the tax for both of them with the coin he found in the mouth of the fish (Mt. 17:27). He passed over a golden opportunity to advocate the non-payment of taxes.

More clear is the well-known teaching of Christ to "render unto Caesar what is Caesar's" (Mk. 12:17). All three Synoptics record this event and its attendant saying (Mk. 12:13-17; Mt. 22:15-22; Lk. 20:20-26). The setting depicts an intentional effort to trap Jesus in some inconsistency, this time trying to pit loyalty to Israel against obedience to the civil magistrate.[122] The Herodians and Pharisees inquire: "Is it right to pay taxes to Caesar or not?" (Mt. 22:15) The implication is that some contemporaries of Jesus did not believe it was *orthos* to pay taxes to Caesar. Most likely, Jewish nationalists who detested Roman imposition advocated tax resistance.[123] Jesus

---

[122] Norval Geldenhuys summarizes the dilemma: ". . . after he had presented himself as the Messiah at the entry . . . He could not possibly reply that the tribute should be given, for then he would lose all hold on the masses (who above all regarded the Messiah as one who would break off the Roman yoke from the people). So the object of their question was to compel him to give an answer that would enable them to accuse him to the Romans of incitement to insurrection." Norval Geldenhuys, *New International Commentary on the New Testament: The Gospel of Luke* (Grand Rapids: Eerdmans, 1979), 503. Cf. also, Oscar Cullmann, op. cit., 34-37.

[123] William Hendriksen elaborates: "The tribute to which the present passage refers was a poll tax which, after the deposition of Archelaus (AD 6), was collected by the procurator from every adult male in Judea, and was paid directly into the imperial treasury. Since this coinage bore the image of the emperor, who ascribed divinity to himself and claimed to possess supreme authority not only in political but even in spiritual affairs . . . it reminded the Jews that they were a

knew the intent of their question (v. 18), and responded in both deed and word. He requested that a denarius, the common currency (Mt. 22:19-20), be brought to him. He then asked, "Whose portrait is this? And whose inscription?" The answer was obviously, "Caesar." Following this lesson in deed, Jesus said: "Give to Caesar what is Caesar's, and to God what is God's" (Mt. 22:22).

The lessons in this one saying, of course, are manifold. Among them, suffice it to note the following. *First,* Jesus admitted that the payment of taxes to the civil government—even if not necessarily a godly administration—is proper. The government is permitted to make coinage and even to put its own symbols on such. Payment of government taxes, in principle, is supported by Jesus. *Second,* by this statement, Jesus implies a limitation to both spheres; neither may rightly usurp the other. *Third,* there is a division of labor. Another legitimate receiver of revenue (as well as honor and obedience) is the treasury of God. Believers are to pay their tithes, as well. Neither of these legitimate spheres necessarily conflict. A century and a half ago (1850), Joseph A. Alexander commented:

> Of the numerous specific senses put upon that answer there are probably but two exegetically possible and yet essentially unlike. The first of these supposes Christ to represent the two things as essentially distinct and independent of each other, belonging to eccentric incommensurable spheres, and therefore not to be reduced to any common principle or rule. As if he had said, Pay your taxes and perform your religious duties, but do not mix the two together or attempt to bring them either into conflict or agreement; for they really belong to different worlds or systems, and have nothing in common or alike by which they can even be compared. . . . The

---

subject nation . . . It was in connection with the introduction of this imposition that Judas of Galilee had vehemently proclaimed, 'Taxation is no better than downright slavery.'" Hendriksen also notes that the denarii contained an image of the ruler with this ascription: Tiberius Caesar Augustus, Son of the Divine Augustus; with the reverse side portraying a throne honoring the emperor as the *Pontif maxim* (high priest). William Hendriksen, *The Gospel of Luke* (Grand Rapids: Baker, 1978), 901-903. Cf. also Norval Geldenhuys, *New International Commentary on the New Testament: The Gospel of Luke* (Grand Rapids: Eerdmans, 1979), 507.

other exegetical hypothesis supposes Christ to say precisely the opposite of this, to wit, that the two duties are in prefect harmony and rest on one and the same principle. . . . Without enumerating . . . it will be sufficient to state two [theories] which can be reduced to this class. The former understands our Lord as rather distinguishing the two obligations, but affirming their constancy and equal obligation, when they are not in collision. The latter understands him as identifying both as parts of one and the same system, as if he had said, your civil duties are but parts of your religious duties. By rendering to Caesar what is his, you render unto God what is his.[124]

Ideally, the jurisdictions should be kept separate; both should be supported by the disciples of Christ. This separation of legitimate scope, however, is not to be encroached. Jesus does not allow for "Caesar" to collect what belongs to "God"; nor for religious groups to assume the role of civil taxation. Both are appropriate in their own places. Taxation, therefore, like civil government in general, is legitimate as long as it is in its proper place and under proper authority.

Of course, this pericope alone does not answer every question about taxation. Questions about relative rates and legitimate uses of taxation must be decided based on this saying along with other revealed truths. Questions about such matters should be answered by the Christian as he or she would resolve other complex matters: not as an individual alone, but as an accountable member of the Body of Christ under tangible authority. Jesus' saying here is sufficient to aid believers in ascertaining that the spheres of government (civil and ecclesiastical) are preserved in their fundamental integrity.

Oscar Cullmann and others conclude that Jesus' teaching on matters of state is essentially compatible with that of Paul and the later New Testament teachings.[125] Cullmann drew three consequences from this harmonious perspective. In sum, they are:

---

[124] Joseph A. Alexander, *The Gospel According to Luke* (rpr. Grand Rapids: Baker, 1980), 327-328.

[125] Oscar Cullmann, *The State in the New Testament* (New York: Charles Scribner's Sons, 1956), 56.

1) Jesus did not regard the state as a "final institution to be equated somehow with the Kingdom of God. The state belongs to the age which still exists even now, but which will definitely vanish as soon as the Kingdom of God comes. Accordingly Jesus' disciples have both the right and the duty to judge the state . . . As long as this age still continues, however, the *existence* of the state is willed by God . . . although it is not of divine nature. Consequently it is not the business of the disciple of Jesus to assume the initiative in abolishing this state as an institution. Rather he is to give the state what it needs for its existence. If, however, the state demands more than is necessary to its existence, as soon as it demands what is God's—thus transgressing its limits—the disciple of Jesus is relieved of all obligation to *this* requirement of a totalitarian state. According to Jesus' command, he is not allowed to give to a state what is God's. But he will not deny even to a totalitarian state those things, like taxes, which are necessary to the existence of any state." At the point of emperor worship, the disciple of Jesus "has to proclaim that the state has transgressed it limits and has demanded what belongs to God . . ."

2) Jesus did not "regard the existing Roman state as an ultimate divine institution." He radically "divorces himself from the Zealots insofar as they intend to establish the Kingdom on their own by human strength . . . They have a false expectation of the Kingdom . . . If the Zealots succeed in realizing their ideal, it will be a totalitarian state of the most extreme form." Jesus admonished the Zealots: "Give the Roman Caesar what is his; therefore do not make a political state out of the community which is to proclaim the Kingdom." If a state "demands what belongs to God the disciple of Jesus has to make this illegitimate trespass known on the basis of the Gospel of Jesus, and he dare not give the state what is God's; he dare not, for example, advocate a doctrine which sets idols in God's place. But even in this case the community of the disciples of Jesus does not have to launch a holy war. Waging war may be a matter for the state, but not for the community of the disciples."[126]

---

[126] Cullmann, op. cit., 50-54.

3) The Roman state in the crucifixion of Jesus did not require worship of the state; thus in its condemnation of Jesus, the state did not exhibit totalitarian excess. Rather it exhibited poor judicial capacity and immoral judgment. In *The State in the New Testament*, Cullmann formulated: "The state appears as something provisional. For this reason we do not find anywhere in the New Testament a renunciation of the state as such as a matter of principle; but neither do we find an uncritical acceptance—as if the state itself were something final, definitive."[127]

Neither Jesus nor the New Testament call for the Christian to be truant in his duty to bring good influence to the state. Doug Bandow writes:

> Christians should infuse the political process, as well as all other human institutions, with biblical values. For reliance on these principles is necessary for a human society that respects religious freedom to exist. As Richard John Neuhaus has observed, 'The force of virtue was thought to be both prior to and reinforcing of the polity. The polity presupposed a culture of virtue; it was not intended to replace it and it could not create a new one in its place.' . . . [However,] investing government with untrammeled coercive power and attempting to turn it, a human organization, into a redemptive instrument is, in essence, to create and worship an ungodly idol.[128]

Christians should not merely be in favor of limiting government; they should also be engaged in moral reform of the platforms underneath government. William Bennett has employed this analogy: "If a victim has been stabbed, pulling out the knife alone will not heal the person. Getting government out of our lives will not *ipso facto* lead to a rebirth of a republican virtue."[129] Christians must follow the political teachings of Jesus in public policy. Jesus did not

---

[127] Ibid., 5.

[128] Doug Bandow, *Beyond Good Intentions* (Wheaton: Crossway, 1988), 117-118.

[129] William J. Bennett and Dan Coats, "Moving Beyond Devolution," *The Wall Street Journal*, Sept. 5, 1995.

call for an abandonment of the public square, but a patient re-clothing. His chosen methods are to use individuals, families, charities, and the church to saturate values.

Christ's teachings have timeless principles and great promise. While many responsibilities are directed to the individual, the church is also the lasting incarnation of Christ as a transforming agent for society and politics. Abraham Kuyper observed,

> Christianity conceals in its womb a much greater treasure of rejuvenation than you surmise. Until now it has exerted its power only on the individual and only indirectly on the state. But anyone who, as believer or as unbeliever, has been able to spy out its secret dynamic, must grant that Christianity can exert a wonderful organizing power on society also; and not till this power breaks through will the religion of the cross shine before the whole world in all the depths of its conception and in all the wealth of the blessings which it brings.[130]

A fine balance is summarized by Doug Bandow:

> Christians should be politically involved. But as believers enter the policy-making process they must be careful to advance genuine biblical standards when they are claiming to represent a Christian perspective. Believers must be especially careful to eschew the temptation to declare God behind every item on their personal political agenda, using their religious affiliation to advance positions that have little or not spiritual dimension. There are, in fact, political controversies that cannot be decided with reference to specific Scriptures; in such cases, the issue can be framed by biblical principles . . .[131]

Other Assumptions of Legitimacy

Many other NT passages mention aspects of civil government. One may ask legitimately: In view of the fact that they are not

---

[130] Abraham Kuyper, *Christianity and the Class Struggle* (Grand Rapids: Piet Hein, 1950), 17.

[131] Doug Bandow, *Beyond Good Intentions* (Wheaton: Crossway, 1988), 119.

overturned demonstrates, does that not at least show the implicit acceptance of Jesus? These other assumptions of legitimacy include the following.

On numerous occasions, Jesus placed his imprimatur on the continuing validity of the OT law. In the Sermon on the Mount, he stated twice that he was not antithetically related to the OT moral law (Mt. 5:17-18). Toward the conclusion of that sermon, he referred to the Golden Rule as summing up the Law and the Prophets (Mt. 7:12). Still later, the two tables of the Law are discernible in his reference to the two great commandments (Mt. 22:34ff.). In conversation with an inquirer Jesus did not avoid stating the demands of the law (Mt. 22:18-19); he reiterated nearly every one. Thus, it is not an easy task to prove that Jesus called for the repudiation of the OT moral standards. Even though he did not advocate an earthly theocracy, he maintained the highest respect for the continuing value of the law in both ethics and politics. As citizens consider legislation and governmental structures, therefore, a recognition of this continuity is necessary.

Jesus tangentially touched on the subject of capital punishment in several places, never calling for its overthrow. In Matthew 15:4, he spoke of the OT prescriptions for capital punishment in violations of the fifth commandment (Mk. 7:10). In this context where he was upbraiding the Pharisees for their novel interpretations, he appears to side with the explicit formulations given to Moses; but he did not overturn the death penalty for serious crimes. Of course, neither did he attempt to institute the death penalty for violations of the fifth commandment.

In various passages, free enterprise and profit are not condemned. In Matthew 20:1-15, Jesus issued a parable about an owner paying differing amounts without mandating the same wage. Commerce may preserve certain market forces without the government calling for identical wages. Wages for honest work are, however, condoned. In fact, in Romans 6:23 the legitimacy of a wage is explicitly recognized. In Luke, Jesus told a parable about a banker who was permitted both to make profit on capital, as well as to lend it out or cancel the debt (Lk. 7:41-42). In another place, our Lord did not condemn interest on deposit with bankers (Mt. 25:27). The conclusion of that parable also shows that an owner may dispense his properties as he sees fit. Thus, the free ownership and use of property, assets, and employees is depicted as acceptable to Jesus. With many features resembling a market-based economy, it is difficult to construe Jesus teaching that free-market economies are inherently sinful; even if he does not explicitly endorse a specific kind of economy. The state which takes wisdom seriously will be careful to structure its own economy within the parameters of what Christ taught as acceptable. Similarly, well-ordered states will not condemn that which Jesus allows, nor mandate that which he prohibits.

Incarceration of prisoners is also a valid function of civil government. When John the Baptist was in prison (Mt. 11:2), Jesus respected punitive institutions. He did not try to help John escape, nor call on his disciples to destroy prisons. Guards are mentioned in the gospels (Mt. 27:15) without criticism of their vocation. Jesus supported punishment of criminals and the use of the sword by the lawful civil agents.

He also recognized the need for legal divorce. In Matthew 19:3-9, he criticized the current laxity among some, but admitted—in accord with the OT—that whenever divorce occurs, legal documentation is appropriate.

Moreover, he spoke of "wars and rumors of wars," never implying that fallen humanity would be altruistic. Jesus even prophesied (Mt. 24:7) that "Nation will rise against nation, and kingdom against kingdom," without criticizing such. He did not call his disciples to pacifism, but acknowledged war as a possibility. Of course, neither did Jesus condone every war, nor did he justify unwarranted aggression.

None of this, however, should minimize his positive teaching that there were occasions for non-retaliation. He exhorted his disciples that times would come in which they would officially be persecuted but not to retaliate (Mt. 10:18-20); instead, they were to flee if at all possible. In his Sermon on the Mount, he taught that disciples were to "turn the other cheek" and "Give to the one who asks," rather than to rudely, defiantly, or selfishly refuse to obey or help (Mt. 5:39-44). In his last moments, when he was struck, he did not retaliate (Jn. 18:10-11). For the Christian, there are times to surrender goods and suffer inconvenience. These alone do not justify retaliation (Rom. 12:17-21).

For those in leadership positions, Jesus did not advocate retreat from public service or from the world. However, he regulated the leadership *ethos*, calling for a servant style of leadership. It was Jesus who said, "The greatest among you must be your servant" (Mt. 23:11). The temptations to arrogance which accompany positions of state are not new. Jesus mandated that his followers adopt a radically different style of leadership which was in stark contrast to the power-mongers of the day (Mt. 20:25; Mk. 10:41-45). Rather than exercising power in arrogance like the non-believing nations, Jesus taught that leaders were to see themselves as servants (Mt. 20:25-27). This diaconal or ministerial style of leadership is reflected in the very appellations adopted by many European governmental departments: as, for example in Italy, the various departments of government are called "The Ministry of Justice," "The Ministry of Defense," etc. Christ taught that whoever led should do so with an attitude of service, rather than seeking to be served (Mt. 20:27).

Such style of civic leadership is in dramatic contrast with Pilate (Mt. 27:14ff.) and others (Jn. 11:45-53), who seem to value expediency, populism, and continuation in office higher than service. An enduring test for those who serve in civil offices is to keep from departing from the standard of service.

It would be incomplete to fail to mention that Jesus actually endorsed few state initiatives. He supported the state in its due claim regarding taxation, regulation of currency, judicial incarceration, waging war, permitting commerce, and making laws. However, he did not advocate manifold large bureaucratic programs to attain those ends. While he accepted a relatively small government, Jesus nowhere taught that the state should regulate commerce, set minimum wages, confiscate personal property, or provide medical care, education, jobs, welfare payments, or environmental hygiene.

It is true that the apparatus of the state in Jesus' time was rather small. Moreover, it remains unproven that smaller governing units are inferior to modern leviathans.

Jesus consistently stressed the responsibility of family members and individuals to care for themselves and others. This earlier age emphasized responsibility in much greater degree than many countries do today. Simultaneously, Christ also called for mercy, charity, and concern for the poor. But the agency appointed to carry out most of these aspects was not the state. Helmut Thielicke has opined:

> It is conceivable that the modern threat to human society, to put it bluntly, arises less from chaos than from an overabundance of state order, a political superorganization which acts as an institutional buffer to isolate men from one another, depersonalize them, forestall direct I-Thou relationships and turn love of neighbor into a welfare machine. The problem can perhaps be clarified in terms of the parable of the Good Samaritan . . . Does not the Samaritan's ministry of mercy become inconceivable, is it not altered in its very substance, the moment it is institutionalized, put into the hands of a 'Good Samaritans' League', e.g., or even into the hands of the state itself? Is it not thereby robbed of its very point? . . . Can the good Samaritan be envisaged as a welfare officer?"[132]

Indeed, something fundamental is altered when the state seeks to perform the duty of the individual, the family, or the church—whether it is doing so under abdication of responsibility by the other legitimate agencies or whether it has usurped their domains. Jesus nowhere advocated statism. Along this same line, F. Edward Payne points out two fallacies resident in confusing compassion with governmental provision of, e.g., medicine.

> First, government programs have been equated with charity. Note that the Bible passages . . . call for *individual* charity, not government programs. Other texts (e.g., 1 Timothy 5:3-16) call for

---

[132] Helmut Thielicke, *Theological Ethics: Politics* (Grand Rapids: Eerdmans, 1979), vol. 3, 291-292.

charity from the church. The reason is simple. *Charity, by definition, is voluntary. Payment of taxes (to give to the "unfortunate") is not voluntary.* Neither the individual nor church has any control over how the money is spent once taxes are paid. Second, nowhere does the Bible give the state the role of charity. . . . Thus, proponents who claim that God has given a role to the government as a charitable institution have no support either from the Bible or from any definition of charity as a voluntary and directed gift.[133]

These distinctions are essential for a consistently Christian view of the state, as well as for the avoidance of harmful effect on society. Isn't one aided in political matters by heeding the counsel of Christ on these matters? Only the worst kind of hubris would be unwilling to listen to Christ's teaching on matters of state or pressing social problems.

Jesus and Poverty

A note of dissent from much contemporary discussion must be issued here about the relative amount of attention Jesus gave to the subject of poverty. A less-ideological review—contrary to the predominant modern liberal perception of Jesus as a glorified Social-Worker *cum* political-activist-advocate for the oppressed—reveals that Jesus did not continually discuss the poor and empowerment themes. From the Gospel corpus few teachings of Jesus normatively address the treatment of the economically poor. That may come as a surprise to many who have been taught otherwise, but a sober study of the matter will bear that out. In fact, only about ten distinct teachings of Christ from the Gospels directly use the word "poor" in an economic sense. When this is recalled, it is perhaps more than anything a sign of the pervasive ideology of social liberalism that the common image of Jesus (as being nearly

---

[133] See F. Edward Payne's "Welfare and Medical Care" in *Welfare Reformed: A Compassionate Approach* (Phillipsburg, NJ: Presbyterian & Reformed, 1994), 183-184.

obsessed or primarily concerned with the materially disadvantaged) is so widespread. It may be the case that Jesus has been conformed to the norms of the statist "Great Society," and the corresponding Gospel accounts read through this filter, rather than culture being judged by the standards of Christ. If one allows Jesus to speak for himself, priorities different from some evangelical treatises may be ascertained.

In agreement with the OT norms, there is a New Testament distinction between the poor in "spirit" and the physically poor (Mt. 5:3). The same phraseology in Luke 6:20 leads most to view "the poor in spirit" as those who recognize or humbly admit their own spiritual inability and ineffectiveness. The spiritually poor include the materially disadvantaged and even the materially wealthy who are Christians. Further, in 2 Corinthians 8:9, Christ himself is spoken of as poor in a sense—probably not a reference to his economic disadvantage, but a reference to the loss and lack he suffered in abandoning his glory in heaven. Revelation 3:17 also speaks of a type of person, who is not poor materially but is impoverished in terms of spiritual health.

Still, in the midst of the above, the economically poor are distinguished as objects worthy of Christ's ministry. In Matthew 11:5, Jesus singled out certain disadvantaged groups of the genuine needy, i.e., the blind, the lame, the leprous, the deaf as those to whom the gospel is preached (cf. also the companion verse in Lk. 7:22). For Jesus, the poor are not invisible. Indeed the church is to care for the poor—just as in the OT. Even in Jesus' own time, certain benevolent customs had been established to ameliorate this problem. Matthew 6:1-4, for example, assumes the giving to the needy. It was a given that the Jewish synagogue would be involved with remediation of the needs of the poor. Jesus taught—not as a higher principle but as a basic assumption—that his disciples would helpfully assist the poor. Jesus neither altered nor originated the duty of believer to care for the poor.

Jesus taught the persistence (non-solubility) of poverty in this world (chiefly, the explicit Mt. 26:11 and Mk. 14:7; cf. also Dt. 15:11). Governmental norms should factor that poverty, according to Jesus' magisterial saying, is not expected to be totally or effectively eliminated in this life. That it will always be a problem affects the levels of expectation and the goals of any state program. For example, if one targets, full employment, total health care, nationalized health insurance, and the abolition of incomes below a certain annual figure, that will substantially alter the extent of state activity as compared to an approach which stresses personal responsibility and familial productivity.

A recognition of God's providence, without the shirking of personal responsibility, might be an important non-economic factor to be included in poverty relief. If it is recalled that the end-targets of state subsidies will largely affect the means of welfare, then these matters should be included as principles. Specifically, if poor people are taught that: wealth is not guaranteed by the state, nor any other source; wealth/health are not "rights"; wealth is not the only factor for human dignity; wealth is ultimately determined by the will of God—then perhaps the orientation toward personal responsibility will be less greed-motivated.

A fine example of the church's compassion can be seen from 1 Timothy 5 below, another case of the excellence of biblical wisdom to guide questioning citizens today.

Paul, Calvin, Poverty, Welfare, and Another Government (1 Tim. 5:1-16)

First Timothy 5:1-16 is one of those rich passages of biblical wisdom, which has not been attended to enough. If we would concentrate on it more, not only would it help our church life but it also would help in a societal-wide problem that has grown exponentially in the last century and may even accelerate in the future. This passage also instructs a growing church to receive folks on a common analogy: as you would family.

To God's praise his church doesn't have age-ism. I think the reason for that is plain. It's likely because most churches view themselves as family. It is also because younger members genuinely desire to learn from and be mentored by more experienced Christians. And every church has people who can significantly benefit some others.

This passage calls for believers to deal lovingly with older church members and to treat them lovingly as *family* members. That is the principle in this verse: to treat church members as you would family members. One may ask: Is there a good reason that such should not guide us in this important area today?

Both sexes and ages, older and younger are addressed in this passage. All possible age-sex differences are covered by these two verses. In each relationship in the church we're to treat others like we would our parents or siblings. Let me draw two conclusions from this verse. *First*, it is the expectation that each normal church, even when young, will be inter-generational.

About a decade ago, there was a theory in the field of church growth studies called *The Homogeneous Unit Principle*. It goes something like this. "Like-attracts-like"—churches with homogenized units grow fastest. Therefore, when starting a church, if one wants to grow large quickly, he should seek to organize groups around age, class, etc., division. The resulting picture of the church would be one of a social organism composed of isolated circles that seldom or never interact. One might create a tight circle of friendship by that social engineering to be sure, but it would result in segregated groups who could not possibly practice these commands. Something should have clued our crack church growth experts about that danger, if they would review this verse. For, this verse precludes such an expectation about the Church. The church is, by God's own design, to be made up of various age groups, and it is not expected to be monogenerational.

The *second* inference which is drawn from this is that the church is pictured as a family. Fathers, mothers, sisters and brothers are dwelling together in this family. And the command on how to treat one another is founded upon this family portrait. Evidently, God preferred to provide a spiritual family for nurture rather than another fraternity or sorority consisting merely of peers.

Following the opening verses, verses 3-16 then turn their attention to the specific way we are to treat widows. The early church saw that as their—not the federal government's—responsibility. Isn't the Bible a practical Book? No one today would dare single out a particular age or marital status group to address. We would fear the prosecution of the EOE enforcers. As a result we would probably speak in such vague generalities that the widows in the church would not be singled out for help. This is an immensely practical book for today.

The Bible seems to take special interest in widows. As far back as in the OT there is an emphasis on the care of widows.

- Exodus 22:22 says, "Do not take advantage of a widow or orphan."
- Dt. 10:18 declares, "God defends the cause of the fatherless and the widow."
- In Dt. 14 & 24, gleanings were left specifically for widows.
- Dt. 27:19 reads, "Cursed is the man who withholds justice from the alien the fatherless, or the widow."
- Psalm 68:5 explains that God is a "defender of widows."
- Psalm 146:9 "The Lord watches over the alien and sustains. . . the widow."
- Proverbs 15:25: "The Lord tears down the proud man's house, but keeps the widows boundaries intact.
- Isaiah 1:17: "Seek justice, encourage the oppressed . . . plead the case of the widow."
- The OT ends with Mal. 3:5. God "will be quick to testify against sorcerers, adulterers, perjurers . . . those who oppress the widows."

The picture is clear from these verses. This is one [of the few] demographic groups singled out for continual protection and care. The reason is that the abandoned widows in ancient societies were left without resources, protection or welfare. There was no Social Security back then. Interestingly, left handed graduates of a school in Memphis who attended seminary in St. Louis do not qualify to receive government subsidy as a disabled group. Widows and orphans, however, have real needs—and no other ways to provide for themselves.

The New Testament continues to affirm consistently that the church is to care for believing widows. By the time of Acts 6 (no later than 32 AD) widows are receiving supplements from the church's food pantry administered by the deacons. Moreover, James 1:27 defines "pure and undefiled" religious expression as "to look after orphans and widows in their distress and to keep oneself from being polluted by the world."

So, yes, the Bible does single out widows and other classes of people who may not be able to fully care for themselves as worthy of being cared for by the church. Those who are most exposed and most vulnerable—like the unborn, the orphans, the aliens and widows—are to be objects of special compassion by the church. The normal church has widows and aging members as well as youthful ones.

What does that mean to your church?

1. Churches should identify widows with need. Some aren't as needy as others. We ought not insult them if they are self-sufficient nor treat them as helpless. But the church ought to identify genuine need when it is present.
2. Churches ought to begin to prepare in advance to effectively care for these elect ladies. Don't wait until problem is upon you. This will happen, and pure and undefiled religion will seek to minister to them.
3. The deacons and others should care for these following the scriptural model in Acts 6 and here. The requirements are given to prevent abuse. They should be followed by us.

Verses 3-16 then present a rather well-organized effort to care for widows. These verses are concerned with two classes of widows: Older widows (3-10, 16) and Younger widows (11-15).

Consider first at the care and requirements for genuine older widows. This passage speaks of a "list" (v. 9), which would (inferred from other passages) be maintained by the deacons. Again this ministry is too important to be haphazardly shepherded. The church is to organize and keep a list of widows "who are really in need" (v. 3). The widows are to receive "proper recognition" (v. 3) lit., *honor* as in Fifth Commandment—the church is to treat those who are on that list with high regard, with great consideration. They, like the older men above, are to be treated with respect and dignity.

There are some requirements that must be met in order for the widows to receive assistance from the church. Like any other formal ministry of the church—just as there are qualifications for Elders, Bishops, Deacons, and Diaconal assistants, so there are qualifications to be on the widow list. The church is not so porous as to be devoid of qualifications or requirements. The qualifications were first of all, that she had no children or grandchildren to care for her (v. 4). Secondly, the widow was to have a real need (v. 5). If she had sufficient income or resources, she wasn't to drain the treasury that others would need. The Church must guard against this, for all our income belongs to the Lord. Thirdly, she was to be a believing and acting Christian. The early church knew nothing of church membership without actual participation in the fellowship. There was no such thing as an "Inactive or Retired Roll" or widows on the roll who weren't believers. If they were disabled or incapacitated, they were still believers. They were, according to verse 5 to "put her hope in God", i.e., trusting him alone for salvation and to "continue night and day to pray (not now and then) and ask God for help." So yes, there were requirements. Parenthetically, this shows that all members of the church are to share in prayer ministry. If widows cannot teach, give, fix or help, they can pray at home continually.

Note: This is a two way street. Some widows may not be treated well because they are unbearable. Children bear with them anyway, but widows have obligation to be respectable. If the widow is "living for pleasure" (v. 6) and not actively loving God and putting her hope in God, then she is not to be on the list. There is a requirement to have an active, growing, praying Christian life if one is cared for by the church.

Next the widow is to have been involved previously in the life and ministry of the church. Verses 9-10 give those qualifications. Yes, there is an age stipulation—over 60. Most of us would not be so brave as to state a specific age, lest one be viewed as discriminatory or ageist. According to this teaching, the widow is to have been maritally faithful to her husband. If not, she may forfeit her place on the aid list. Verse 10 describes her life of ministry in these areas to be proven. The church widow is to be:

- Well known for good deeds in general.
- Bringing up her children to be Christians.
- Showing hospitality.
- Washing the feet of the saints—this is a Metaphor for lowly service to Christians.
- Helping those in trouble.
- Devoting herself to all kinds of good deeds.
  So IF a woman is:

- Over 60.
- Faithful to husband.
- A believing, praying Christian.
- With no children or grandchildren to care for her.
- Has a real need as determined by deacons.
- She's proven herself in these areas of service

THEN, it is mandated that she be put on a list to be cared for. To be on the list is a reward for lifelong Christian service. If the church does not care for them when they have real needs, then we're not much of a church and our religion is not "pure and undefiled" (James 1:27). We should thankfully honor the older women and older men in our church as our parents and grandparents . . . in the faith. It is a privilege and calling of God. We are greatly indebted to them.

There are certain timeless principles, which are clear here. If followed—even on a national scale—might we not be better off? Good biblical principles on the care of widows are also applicable in caring for the needy.

Here in four derived principles is guidance for biblical reform for welfare or social relief in general.

1. There are requirements, which must be met to qualify for this welfare. If there is a more basic care unit (family) or if there is capacity for industry, then those are to be used first. They provide an initial sorting out.
2. The family is the primary unit to care for older people's welfare. Welfare is not a bad word. It's just how it's used. The biblical view is that God ordained the family to care for one another. The Fifth Commandment to honor Father and Mother is still binding today. We in the Christian family are to care for older family members ourselves and not shirk that responsibility. This passage teaches the first layer of responsibility is family. Verse 8 even teaches that to neglect providing for one's family is to deny the faith and be worse than an unbeliever. *Don't let pagans show you up.*
3. The church, not the state, (not even mentioned) is to be the second layer of welfare. When families aren't available to care for older people that concern devolves to the church. The church is to care for its widows. This means funds and material assistance must be made available.
4. Younger widows are to seek (v. 16) to be useful. If you can work then be productive.

Think of a drug-dealing young mother, Phyllis. A Christian meets her and she asks the Christian for money. The Christian asks what for, and she says, "For food." The Christian says that he won't give her money but he will take her to a cafe and buy her a meal. He tells her where she may get a meal daily supplied by the Salvation Army. While they eat he tells her of salvation in the Lord Jesus Christ. Phyllis is noncommittal. A week later she returns and asks for money again but the Christian says to her, "I will buy food for you again, but if you want us to continue to help you, you will have to let us into your life." Phyllis asks what he means. "I mean that there may be habits and patterns in your life that are pulling you down and are the cause of your being out of money again. If we in the church are going to truly help you, we need to look at your whole life. You may need help in managing your pension, paying your rent, buying food and weaning you away from playing bingo every day of your life. It would not be truly loving of us simply to give you money or even buy you food unless you let us help you more extensively." At that Phyllis got angry and got up and walked out. Her life was her business, and she never returned.

It is our love for them that sets limits on the mercy that we show them. Because we love them we have to say no to giving them money for drugs, for drink, for bingo. It would be unloving to give them money for such self-destruction. They need to feel the full consequences of their own irresponsibility. We say, "Phyllis, we will still pray for you, and visit you. The moment you are willing to cooperate with us and make the changes that are needed we can give you practical help. It is only out of love that we are now saying No to your request for money." Our love for them limits our mercy.

Calvin on Welfare

One of the stalwart aids in mature reflection on a subject like this is the employment of church history as a corroborating guide to the subject. In what follows, I would like to present some of the principles and practices of welfare from a period nearly five centuries ago. One assumption is that over even long periods of time the human condition and social solutions are basically constant. Therefore, is one wise to fail to benefit from what has successfully worked in other eras? This study highlights some of the best practice from on Protestant tradition. In our survey we concentrate on the contribution to the diaconate by John Calvin and others from the reformed tradition.

The Bourse Francaise became a pillar of societal welfare;[134] indeed, this was one of Calvin's contributions to Western civilization. This diaconal ministry may have had nearly as much influence in Calvin's Europe as his theology did in other areas.

---

[134] Jeannine Olson, *Calvin and Social Welfare: Deacons and the Bourse Francaise* (Cranbury, NJ: Susquenhanna University Press), 11-12.

Calvin's welfare program in Geneva was contoured to the theological emphases of the reformers, providing an earlier illustration that welfare practice was and is (and still should be) erected upon definite principles that were religious or ideological in nature. Moreover, the theology of the Reformation was the guiding force for this welfare, just as the theology of medieval Roman Catholicism was the guiding principle for almsgiving. Ultimate principles contoured the practice of welfare 450 years ago as they do today, which is to say, that at no time is welfare truly divorced from underlying ideological values.

Of course, the Genevan model for welfare did not claim uniqueness; rather, it viewed itself as the culmination of a number of factors. Among other precedents, it saw itself built upon the earlier texts of the OT, the *Acts* narratives, and earlier canonical precedents (e. g., the Synod of Tours in 567 which assigned the responsibility of caring for the poor to each parish priest) describing the work of the diaconate. Thus the Bourse saw itself as standing on the shoulders of the work of Christians who had preceded.

The activities of the Bourse were numerous. Its diaconal agents were involved in housing orphans, the elderly, or those who were in any way incapacitated. They sheltered the sick, and dealt with orphans and those involved in immoralities. This ecclesiastical institution was a precursor to voluntary societies in the nineteenth and twentieth centuries.

The Bourse Francaise was founded under the leadership of John Calvin sometime between 1536 and 1541 (exclusive of the time of his Strassbourg exile). Its initial design was to appease the suffering brought onto French residents who, while fleeing sectarian persecution in France, came to Geneva. It has been estimated that in that single decade alone (1550-1560) some 60,000 refugees came through Geneva, a number significantly large to produce significant social stress.

Early on in the *Ecclesiastical Ordinances* first proposed in 1541, John Calvin had written a charter for the deacons, distinguishing them as one of the four basic offices. This

Reformation church order stipulated that among the fourth biblical office, that of deacon, "There were always two kinds in the ancient Church, the one deputed to receive, dispense, and hold goods for the poor, not only daily alms, but also possessions, rents and pensions; the other to tend and care for the sick and administer allowances to the poor."[135] In addition, this charter prescribed, "It will be their duty to watch diligently that the public hospital is well maintained, and that this be so both for the sick and the old people unable to work, widowed women, orphaned children and other poor creatures. The sick are always to be lodged in a set of separate rooms from the other people who are unable to work . . . Moreover, besides the hospital for those passing through which must be maintained, there should be some attention given to any recognized as worthy of special charity."[136] In the conclusion of this section, Calvin advocated "to discourage mendicancy which is contrary to good order, it would be well, and we have so ordered it, that there be one of our officials at the entrance of the churches to remove from the place those who loiter; and if there be any who give offence or offer insolence to bring them to one of the Lords Syndic."[137] Begging without honest work was an affront to the biblical Protestant work. With sophistication of administration and discrimination of root causes among physical needs, this model can still inform our practice today.

Calvin was so interested in seeing the diaconate flourish that Calvin not only left an inheritance for his family in his will but also provided for the Boys School and poor strangers.[138] Yet, this Bourse was not an entirely new institution, although its roots were decidedly connected to the theology and the experience of Geneva. The deacons cared for a large range of needs, not wholly dissimilar to the strata of welfare needs in our own society.

---

[135] *Calvin Theological Treatises,* J. K. S. Reid, ed. (Philadelphia: Westminster, 1954), 64.

[136] Ibid., 65.

[137] Ibid., 66.

[138] Cited by Geoffrey Bromiley, "The English Reformers and Diaconate," *Service in Christ* (London: Epworth Press, 1966), 113.

In the 1541 *Ecclesiastical Ordinances* of Geneva, Calvin recommended a strong role for the diaconate, especially in almsgiving. After two decades, those *Ecclesiastical Ordinances* were revised in 1561. The 1561 *Ecclesiastical Ordinances* shows the sophistication and refinement of the diaconate even prior to the death of Calvin.[139] The following sections taken from the 1561 revision make clear that ministry to the poor was significant and well-ordered in Calvin's time. It was neither a low priority nor slip-shod in organization.[140] The Swiss and French Reformed churches were agreed on "The Fourth Order of the Ecclesiastical Government, the Deacons," which was chartered as follows in the 1561 revision:

56.   There were always two kinds in the ancient church: some delegated to receive, dispense and conserve the goods of the poor, daily alms as well as possessions, allowances, and pensions; others to attend to and care for the sick and administer the daily pittance. (It is indeed right for all Christian cities to conform to this, as we have tried to do and intend to continue [doing] in the future.) For we have trustees and hospital administrators; and to avoid confusion, let one of the four trustees of the hospital be the receiver of all the possessions of the above, and let him have funds sufficient to perform his task better.

57.   Let the number of four stewards remain as it has been: one of whom will have charge of receipts, as stated, both that provisions may be laid in more promptly and also that those who wish to give alms to the poor may be more certain that the goods will not be used otherwise than they intended. And if the revenue were not sufficient, or even if it exceeded extraordinary necessity, let the Synod advise adjustment in accordance with the poverty they observe . . .

---

[139] Cf. Mary Crumpacker, "Ecclesiastical Ordinances, 1561," David W. Hall and Joseph H. Hall, eds., *Paradigms in Polity* (Grand Rapids: Eerdmans, 1994), 148-149.

[140] For more on this, cf. my "Calvin's Principles of Governance: Homology in Church and State," in David W. Hall, *Tributes to John Calvin: A Celebration of His Quincentenary* (Phillipsburg, NJ: Presbyterian and Reformed Publishing, 2010), 314-341.

60. It will be necessary to watch carefully that the common hospital is well maintained and that it is as much for the sick as for the elderly who are unable to work, such as widows, young orphans, and other poor. However, the sick shall be kept together in a lodging apart and separated from the others.

61. Item, let the care of the poor who are scattered throughout the city return there as the trustees direct.

62. Item, besides the hospital for transients, which needs to be retained, there shall be some ward apart from those perceived to be especially deserving of charity; and to accomplish this, there shall be a room reserved for their use . . .

64. Let the ministers, commissioners or elders with one of the Syndics take the responsibility for inquiring whether in the above-mentioned administration of the poor there be any fault or indigence, in order to beseech and warn the Synod to settle the matter. And to do this, some of their company with the stewards shall visit the hospital quarterly to ascertain whether all is in good order.

65. It will also be necessary for the poor of the hospital as well as those of the city who have no way of helping themselves to have a doctor and a qualified surgeon on the city's payroll who, even if they practice in the city, were nevertheless engaged to care for the hospital and visit the other poor.

66. And because not only the old and sick are taken to our hospital but also young children because of their poverty, we have ordered that there always be a teacher to instruct them in morality, and in the rudiments of the letters and Christian doctrine. For the most part, he shall catechize, teaching the servants of the aforesaid hospital and conduct the children to the college.

67. As to the hospital for infectious diseases, it shall be entirely separate, especially if the city happens to have been visited by some scourge from God.

68. Moreover, to prevent begging, which is contrary to good order, it will be necessary (and so we have ordered) that the Synod station some of its officers at the exits of the churches to remove those who would like to beg, and if they resist or are recalcitrant to take them to one of the Syndics. Similarly for the rest of the time let the leaders of the groups of ten see to it that the prohibition on begging is well observed.

The deacons actively encouraged a productive work ethic. They provided interim subsidy and job-training as necessary; on occasion, they even provided the necessary tools or supplies so that an able-bodied person could engage in an honest vocation. They were discriminating as they ascertained the difference between the truly needy and the indigent. If necessary, they would also suspend subsidy. Over time, they developed procedures that would protect the church's resources from being pilfered, even requiring new visitors to declare their craft and list character witnesses to vouch for their honesty.[141] Within a generation of this welfare work, the diaconate of Geneva discovered the need to communicate to recipients the goal that they were to return to work as soon as possible.

In sixteenth century Geneva, there were cases of abandonment; the Bourse was frequently called upon to raise children. They supported the terminally ill who also left their children to be supported. Special gifts were given to truly needy children. The Bourse also included a ministry to widows who often had dependent children and a variety of needs.

Still, it must be noted that although the Bourse resembled many other contemporary welfare funds, it had its own peculiarities. Naturally there were theological peculiarities, and these theological distinctives led to certain practical commitments. For example, there were *no guaranteed food hand-outs*. Furthermore (as I note below), there were certain pre-requisites for receiving care, including the possibility that certain moral deficiencies would nullify the opportunity to be assisted by the Bourse.

The Bourse was not concerned only with spiritual or internal needs. On many occasions they hired medical doctors to take care of the ill. Their records indicate that the deacons oversaw medical care for the needy, reflecting that the full scope of diaconal ministry was not limited only to evangelism. Those who led the Bourse were also prudent. By January of 1581, the Bourse adopted

---

[141] Olson, op. cit., 39-40.

a set of constitutional rules underscoring the need to have a vital and well thought out disciplined approach to poverty amelioration.[142]

For our own times it is perhaps instructive to note that in Calvin's era social welfare was not totally egalitarian. Historian Jeannine Olson notes:

> There was an effort in Geneva to maintain the image of the Bourse Francaise as a fund to help people who were considered worthy, rather than as an institution that indiscrimi-nately aided everyone. The funds were intended for those who were in genuine need, particularly those who were ill or handicapped. The deserving poor were numerous in this age before modern medicine or surgery, when a simple hernia or poorly aligned broken bone could render one unable to work. The limited funds of the Bourse were not intended for derelict poor, those who are considered unwilling to work, lazy and slothful vagrants and vagabonds, to use the popular English terminology of the era. The assumption that welfare recipients should be worthy of aid had long been common in Europe, but the definition of worthiness varied from one milieu to another.[143]

Despite the rigor with which the deacons distinguished between the deserving and undeserving poor, charity motivated these to err on the side of generosity. Still, however, there were times and instances in the records of the Bourse when the deacons would not give assistance to those because of attitudinal or moral blights. Charity did not imply a style of giving that mitigated against personal industry and responsibility. There were a number of instances in which if one were to behave immodestly or unchastely then he/she would not receive certain aid. Recipients of subsidy were expected to uphold Christian standards of morality; if not, the Bourse might well withhold support until immoral behavior was jettisoned. The deacons attempted to use the Bourse as a means of discipline and encouragement.

---

[142] Ibid., 104-106.
[143] Ibid., 139.

In comparison, The Heritage Foundation's paper "Understanding Poverty in America," reports the following facts about the "poor" as defined by the U.S. Census Bureau. It provides a good opportunity to consider the subjectivity of the definition of poverty since:

- 46% of the "poor" own their homes;
- 76% have air conditioning;
- Only 6% of the "poor" households are overcrowded;
- The average "poor" American enjoys more square footage of living space than individuals living in Paris, London, Vienna or Athens;
- 97% of the "poor" own a color TV, and 62% have cable or satellite reception;
- 89% of the "poor" report their families have enough to eat, while only 2% say they "often" do not have enough to eat.[144]

Compare the vision of the poor as presented in the Bible—men without homes, bodies full of sores, hungry, owning only one tunic—to the circumstances many of the U. S. poor, and the social skewing of the definition of poverty becomes apparent. Poor often means "having less than my neighbor" instead of "going without."

These five fundamental assumptions about modern poverty relief (which are directly opposed to the theology and spirit of Calvinism) may be questioned for numerous reasons:

1) Poverty can be eliminated.
2) Man has a right to sustenance.
3) Man is not responsible for his economic plight.
4) Compassion does not require accountability and change.

---

[144] Robert E. Rector and Kirk A. Johnson, "Understanding Poverty in America," The Heritage Foundation, January 5, 2004. For an update, see Ryan Messmore, "Does Advocating Limited Government Mean Abandoning the poor?" at: http://www.heritage.org/Research/Reports/2011/05/Does-Advocating-Limited-Government-Mean-Abandoning-the-Poor.

5) Government is the institution best suited to lead the effort.[145]

Of the various impacts, these five premises are highlighted here as a demonstration of an impoverished underlying theology and of the expense that is incurred by all parties involved in the equation—the poor, the relief worker, the government, the non-poor. A complete analysis of these 5 negative results is beyond our scope, but a quick listing of their ill-effects is an argument with self-evidentiary logic. Among those ill-effects are: 1) corruption, 2) inefficiency, 3) the entrenchment of "professional" relief workers and gov-ernmental agencies, 4) the skewing of taxation, and 5) the "politicization" of poverty relief.

In his *Commentaries,* Calvin also consistently set forth similar principles. On 2 Thessalonians 3:10, Calvin commented, "When, however, the Apostle commanded that such persons should not eat, he does not mean that he gave commandment to those persons, but forbade that the Thessalonians should encourage their indolence by supplying them with food . . . Paul censures those lazy drones who lived by the sweat of others, while they contribute no service in common for aiding the human race."[146] In commenting on Psalm 112:9, the Genevan reformer elaborated,

> . . . by dispersing [to the poor], the prophet intimates, that they did not give sparingly and grudgingly, as some do who imagine that they discharge their duty to the poor when they dole out a small pittance to them, but that they give liberally as necessity requires and their means allow; for it may happen that a liberal heart does not possess a large portion of the wealth of this world . . . Next he adds, they give to the poor, meaning that they do not bestow their charity at random, but with prudence and discretion meet the wants of the necessitous. We are aware that unnecessary and superfluous expenditure for the sake of ostentation is frequently lauded by the world; and consequently, a larger quantity of the good things of this life is squandered

---

[145] For more on this, see David W. Hall and Matthew D. Burton, *Calvin and Commerce* (Phillipsburg, NJ: Presbyterian and Reformed, 2009), 135-149 .

[146] *Calvin's Commentaries (*rpr. Grand Rapids: Baker, 1979), vol. xxi, 355.

away in luxury and ambition than is dispensed in charity prudently bestowed. The prophet instructs us that the praise which belongs to liberality does not consist in distributing our goods without any regard to the objects upon whom they are conferred, and the purposes to which they are applied, but in relieving the wants of the really necessitous, and in the money being expended on things proper and lawful.[147]

Thus the experiment in welfare in Geneva offers a clinic in what may happen when welfare is conformed to biblical impulses.

It is helpful to remember also that the Bourse Francaise was a transitional institution. Occurring at the consummation of centuries of medieval welfare, yet renewed by the Protestant Reformation, the founders of the Bourse did not hold to the utopian notion that poverty would be entirely eliminated. In reference to Jesus' statement in Mark 14:7 ("you will always have the poor with you"), these founders of the Genevan Diaconate were realists who consulted the past as they formed new manifestations of earlier models. As reformers they were most attracted to the institution of the early church, finding that model most fruitful for their reforms. These reformers lived on a cusp of a reform movement, learning from what had gone before them.

As those who look to the past and to the inadequacies of the present, perhaps we should replicate some of that posture, too. Might we be better off from this and other studies to see what we can learn from the past, rather than looking exclusively to the future? In fact, if we find ourselves advocating practices markedly different from what the Bourse in Geneva did nearly five centuries ago, then it may be that our novel methods should be suspect to the extent that we deviate from earlier sound practice in the area of public welfare.

In summary thus far, we have seen the following as principles of Reformation welfare reform:

1) It was only for the truly disadvantaged.

---

[147] *Calvin's Commentaries* (rpr. Grand Rapids: Baker, 1979), vol. vi., 328-329.

2) Moral prerequisites accompanied assistance.
3) Private or religious charity, not state largesse, was the vehicle for aid.
4) Ordained officers managed and brought accountability.
5) Theological underpinnings were normal.
6) Productive work ethic was sought.
7) Assistance was temporary.
8) History is valuable.

In a sermon on 1 Timothy 3:8-10, Calvin associated the early church's compassion as the canon to measure our Christianity: "When there were neither lands nor possessions nor what is called property of the church, it was necessary that each give his offering and from that the poor be supplied. If we want to be considered Christians and want it to be believed that there is some church among us, this organization must be demonstrated and maintained." Later in that same sermon he enjoined, "Now when that property has been distributed as it ought, if that still does not meet all needs, let each give alms privately and publicly, so that the poor may be aided as is fitting.

The testimony of Calvin is quite full. In one of his sermons on 1 Timothy 3:8-13, he remarked:

> We saw this morning what position St. Paul discusses here, that is, that of those who in the ancient church were ordained to distribute the alms. It is certain that God wants such a rule observed in His church: that is, that there be care for the poor— and not only that each one privately support those who are poor, but that there be a public office, people ordained to have the care of those who are in need so that things may be conducted as they ought. And if that is not done, it is certain that we cannot boast that we have a church well-ordered and according to the gospel, but there is just so much confusion. [148]

Later in the same source, Calvin commented, "And yet the deacons are those ordained to have the care of the poor and to distribute

---

[148] Ibid., 183.

alms, the care not only of distributing what is entrusted to them, but of inquiring where there is need and where the property ought to be used ... We must find people who may govern the property of the poor. These are the sacrifices offered to God today, that is, alms. Therefore it is necessary that they be distributed by those whom God considers suitable for such a position, and that the deacons who are chosen *should be as the hands of God*, and be there in a holy office."[149] So strong was Calvin's view that he preached,

> Inasmuch as it is a question of the spiritual government which God has put among His own, St. Paul wants those who are ordained, whether to proclaim the gospel or to have the care of the poor, to be of irreproachable life ... We must carefully note these passages where it is proclaimed to us what order God has established in His Church, so that we may take care to conform ourselves to it the best we can ... Because if we want to have the Church among us, we must have this government which God has established as inviolable, or at least we must strive to conform ourselves to it.[150]

Calvin, whose name is not always and immediately identified with compassionate advocacy for welfare to the poor, even on one occasion rhetorically asserted, "Do we want to show that there is reformation among us? We must begin at this point, that is, there must be pastors who bear purely the doctrine of salvation, and then deacons who have the care of the poor."

Commenting on Romans 12:8, another nearby reformer John Oecolampadius made this point about deacons and ministry to the poor:

> Sixth, those who show mercy, who differ in this way. For those who give mutually, and form their own means supply the hungry and the naked, are said to impart. And these ought to give simply and freely, without respect for temporal concerns, or friendship,

---

149 Ibid., 184.
150 Idem.

or convenience. Those indeed who visit the sick and captives and are present with the afflicted are called those who show mercy, and their office ought to be done with a cheerful spirit and with promptness. Seventh are those who preside in any congregation; these ought to be courteous and diligent . . .[151]

Elsie McKee summarizes the Genevan practice as follows:

Two or three things about most Protestants' almsgiving are notably different from the late medieval equivalent. One is the new organization, the coordination and centralization. This, however, was common to Roman Catholic as well as Protestant charity, and became universal. Another point is the matter of the poor begging for alms, whether in church or in the streets. . . . Protestants permitted only designated people to collect alms for the poor . . . A third point, however, the fact that Protestant almsgiving was repeatedly, explicitly or implicitly associated with the central official act of worship, distinguishes it from sixteenth century Roman Catholicism as well as from the late medieval church. Among the great majority of the Reformed churches, an alms collection became part of the regular worship order. . . . The common custom was a collection at the door, and it is probable that at least in a significant number of cases this was associated with a concluding exhortation to remember the poor. It seems probable that Calvin himself collected alms during his Strasbourg Communion service, and it is certain that he believed no person should come before God empty-handed. . . . At least for the Reformed tradition, an adequate understanding of the relationship of worship and benevolence can be more fully, perhaps, better, achieved by an investigation of the diaconate. It is the doctrine of the diaconate which determines the ecclesiastical or civil nature of charity in the sixteenth century.[152]

The emphases of Calvin lived on after his death. Even one of the adversaries of Theodore Beza (Calvin's disciple), Jean Morely, affirmed a strong role for the church to care for those in poverty. In his 1562 *Treatise on Christian Discipline,* Morely asserted that in

---

[151] Ibid., 191.
[152] Elsie Anne McKee, *John Calvin on the Diaconate and Liturgical Almsgiving* (Geneva: Librarie Droz, 1984), 65.

some organized manner, the church should "relieve the poor, and property should be set aside for its support. For poverty creates temptations to vice and corruption which few can resist. . . . In fact many of the arrangements are designed primarily to keep the able-bodied but indolent poor from receiving aid on a regular basis, so that all the church's resources for poor relief can go to those victims of circumstance who are deserving and helpless"[153]

Of all the reformers, Martin Bucer was considered the "theologian of the diaconate" since he wrote most directly about the function of the church in caring for the poor. Bucer argued in his 1560 *De Regno Christi* that, "there must be in the 'Christian Republic' a thorough organization of poor relief and assistance to the sick . . . for the fulfillment of these ends discipline is essential, and so there must be a thorough organization of labour and leisure."[154]

Bucer went so far as to say of the diaconate that "without it there can be no true communion of saints,"[155] while simultaneously believing that, "The first duty of the deacons is to distinguish between the deserving and undeserving poor, for the former to inquire carefully into their needs; the latter, if they lead disorderly lives at the expense of others, to expel them from the community of the faithful. Care, next, is to be taken for needy widows. The second duty of deacons is to keep a written record of accounts, having sought diligently for the proper collecting of funds from all the parishioners according to their capacity."[156]

In the British Isles, almsgiving was emphasized as one means for poverty relief. King Edward VI would assert that, "to relieve the poor is . . . a true worshiping of God."[157]

---

[153] Cited in Robert M. Kingdon's *Geneva and the Consolidation of the French Protestant Movement, 1564-1572* (Madison, WI: Univ. of Wisconsin Press, 1967), 56.

[154] Basil Hall, "Diaconia in Martin Butzer," *Service in Christ* (London: Epworth Press, 1966), 94.

[155] Ibid, 99.

[156] Idem.

[157] Cited by Geoffrey Bromiley in "The English Reformers and Diaconate," *Service in Christ,* (London: Epworth Press, 1966), 120.

Hence the Calvinistic tradition was settled and fairly uniform in their institutionalization of the care for the poor. It was an ecclesiological function (surely an NGO) to be carried out by spiritual officers according to biblical standards and principles. As it was carried out well, it cared for the poor, employed the church's gifts, encouraged a productive work ethic, and relieved governmental stewardship in this area. As Bromiley summarizes, "the able-bodied should work and support themselves . . . The answer to poverty was still found in individual benevolence exercised either privately or through the Church."[158]

Zurich also was a model for social welfare. The city began its reform and its diaconal ministry as early as 1520. The same may be said for Strassburg and other cities in Lutheran territory. For example, "[i]n Strassburg, preaching of welfare reform began before the Protestant Reformation. Geiler Von Kaysersberg urged a new system of poor relief that included a suggestion that able-bodied people should work. Only those incapable of work, he argued, should receive relief."[159] Remembering that when exiled from Geneva, Calvin spent two years in the late 1530s in Strassburg, it is possible that these other Swiss reformed models could have indeed shaped, in no small part, the welfare relief model of Geneva.

Nor did the other magisterial reformer Martin Luther fail to translate his faith into practice in the area of poverty relief. As early as 1520, in his *Address to the German Nobility*, Luther "strongly disapproved of any and every kind of mendicancy and beggary and advised every town to assume responsibility for its own poor and needy by appointing an official to advise the pastor."[160] Begging was to be eliminated as its erstwhile theological foundation crumbled under Dr. Martin's *sola fides* theology. Begging could no longer be viewed as a monastic ideal, as a meritorious work, nor as Christian perfection. Instead, it was to be curtailed as much as

---

[158] Bromiley, op. cit., 113.

[159] Ibid., 165.

[160] James Atkinson, "Diaconia at the Time of the Reformation," *Service in Christ* (London: Epworth Press, 1966), 84.

possible by a proper theological correction. Begging would be eradicated with the care for the poor assigned to each small unit of governing—the individual city. In his *Babylonian Captivity* (1520), Luther saw the church through its diaconate as the agency to minister to the poor, in contrast to the role of deacons within Roman Catholicism: "The diaconate . . . is a ministry, not for reading the Gospel and the Epistle, as the practice is nowadays, but for distributing the Church's bounty to the poor, in order that the priests might be relieved of the burden of temporal concerns and give themselves more freely to prayer and the Word."[161] In Strasburg, "we find as early as 1523 a thorough evangelical organization under the care of a director, four assistant directors, nine church workers with twenty-one helpers. Here it was stipulated that the poor were not only to be helped materially but to be visited as persons at least four times in a year."[162] Ministry to the poor by the church was not a later development for the reformers.

Luther, it should also be remembered, was opposed to handouts without responsibility or true demonstration of need. He earthily quipped, "Do not spoonfeed the masses. If we were to support Mr. Everybody, he would turn too wanton and go dancing on the ice."[163] According to Luther, the "poor by their own folly" were not deserving of help.

One can also profit from the example of the Roman Catholic humanist, Juan Luis Vives.[164] The major source of his views on social welfare may be found in his 1526 *On the Help of the Poor*. Vives, a product of renaissance humanism, offered a state-of-the-art version of welfare. In that both Vives and the Protestant reformers had drunk deeply from the pedagogy of humanism, in some ways their systems resembled each other's.[165]

---

[161] Ibid., 86.

[162] Idem.

[163] Cited by Geoffrey Bromiley in "The English Reformers and Diaconate" in *Service in Christ* (London: Epworth Press, 1966), 112.

[164] Cf. Abel Athouguia Alves, "The Christian Social Organism and Social Welfare: The Case of Vives, Calvin, and Loyola," *Sixteenth Century Journal*, XX, no. 1, 1989, 3-21.

[165] McKee is in slight disagreement with an aspect of the following study as to

Vives, respected in his day for a range of expertise, applied his talents to the remediation of poverty. He maintained views that may stand out in our own time, but to his contemporaries he was putting forth 'mere' Christian charity. Vives wrote, "I will not have as a Christian he who, within his means, gives no help to an indigent brother."[166] For Vives, "[t]he Christian society, the society which strives for earthly justice, looks to the divine law to be reconstituted as just, thus imitating the self's interaction with grace."[167] Abel Alves and others even trace many of the poverty relief laws enacted in Spain in the 1520s and 1530s to the influence of Vives on these matters. So decidedly Christian was Vives' method that he drew attack from the rival secularists who preferred to follow Machiavelli. Vives advocated the impact of the principles of Christian morality on welfare and believed that the "'lay' urban social organism was to be a reflection of Christian morality."[168]

Along with Loyola he affirmed the propriety of catechetical instruction as a part of any Christian-based welfare, along with the

---

the importance of Vives. In her discussion of the origins of social welfare in the Reformation era, she confirms what we have seen above, although she disputes the original contributions of Vives:

> "Where did the welfare reform begin and who influenced whom? The two major contenders for priority are certain cities of Germany and the Netherlands. A third suggestion which has called forth heated argument is that of the humanist Juan L. Vives, whose book *De subventione pauperum* (1526) was thought to have been the model for many cities. It has been fairly conclusively proved that Vives was not the father of sixteenth-century welfare reform though he was a popular and able exponent of the new movement. Having eliminated Vives, the chief candidates for first place are the German city of Nuremberg and the Flemish city of Ypres. The case for the latter is weakened by the elimination of Vives, who was thought to have outlined the Ypres reform. In fact, as the majority of scholars now affirm, Ypres is more like Nuremberg than like Vives' model, and the chronology of the wave of reform spreading across France, Italy, Spain, and England, lends weight to the claim that South Germany was the point of origin" (101, *John Calvin on the Diaconate and Liturgical Almsgiving, supra*).

[166] Cited by Alves, op. cit., 8.

[167] Ibid.

[168] Ibid., 14.

administration of fines to punish professional beggars.[169] He may even have predated by four and a half centuries Pope John XXIII, who stressed the family basis of welfare.

> The family, grounded on marriage freely contracted, monogamous and indissoluble, must be considered the first and essential cell of human society. To it must be given, therefore, every consideration of an economic, social, cultural, and moral nature which will strengthen its stability and facilitate the fulfillment of its specific mission.[170]

Vives' method is summarized by Alves:

> The methods of his proposed system included a division of the poor into deserving native elements and undeserving foreign beggars; the establishment of work programs; and the generation of relief revenue through donations, the earnings of the poor's labor, and the use of money previously spent by the city on frivolous festivals. . . . poor relief necessarily resulted from the Christian organic concept, but the Christian social thinker knew in advance that the ideal would never function perfectly on earth . . . Vives desired vocational training for young paupers so that they would not always remain impoverished, but he wanted to keep both able-bodied and handicapped adults actively employed at all times to prevent idleness, the devil's playground. Those who were so morally corrupt that they refused to work were to be given just enough food to stay alive; but they were still to be given food.[171]

Vives shared with Calvin and other Protestants the view of depravity that maintained both that the charity-dispensers and the charity-recipients were sinful and therefore must be constrained by order and accountability. Furthermore, "Vives, Calvin, and Loyola all recognized the importance of planned relief. They distinguished

---

[169] Ibid., 15.

[170] Cited by Michael Novak in *Gaining Ground* (Washington, DC: Ethics and Public Policy Center, 1986), 65.

[171] Alves, op. cit., 12-13.

between deserving and undeserving poor, and they all accepted the occasional confinement of the poor to hospitals as a given."[172]

Calvin, and later Beza, "condemned the unwillingness of the wealthy to aid the poor; with Calvin quite clearly stating that reluctance to work tried God's power and patience."[173] Loyola went so far as to construct a scale of punishments for able-bodied beggars, and as an example of the Roman Catholic approach of the time he maintained that "[k]ndness and harsh discipline both [were needed] in actual Christian practices," and that based on the separation of the sheep from the goats in Matthew 25:40, "[t]here had to be deserving and undeserving poor to explain this dichotomy. The sick, disabled, widowed, and orphaned were separated from the sturdy and lazy."[174] In sum, "Social control and social responsibility were inter-woven."

In line with the above two leading puritans made similar comments. William Ames, describing idlesess as the mother of many vices, spoke of:

> the lusty beggards and vagabonds are not to be suffered. Firstly, because they openly oppose themselves to the Divine Ordinance. Secondly, they are a burden to others without necessity. Thirdly because they defraud those who are poor indeed of some part of the alms they would receive if they had not been prevented by such. Fourthly, they do not carry themselves as members of any church or commonwealth. Fifthly, they directly set themselves to many kinds of wickedness.[175]

The views of William Perkins, the leading puritan theologian of the time, were similar to this Reformation tradition:

> . . . rogues, beggars, and vagabonds . . . commonly are of no civil society or corporation; they join not themselves to any settled congregation for the obtaining of God's kingdom; they are (for

---

[172] Ibid., 12.

[173] Ibid., 13.

[174] Idem..

[175] Cf. George Rule, "The Puritans" in *Service in Christ* (London: Epworth Press, 1966), 129.

the most part) a cursed generation.' But as the author of this view, Mr. Christopher Hill, freely admits, there are countless places in Perkins' works which attack covetousness, usury, unjust dealing, and these could hardly be acceptable to the grasping bourgeois members of the congregation which, we are told, heard Perkins preach with avidity. Hill gets over this difficulty by saying that they just did not listen to those bits. Self-deception does indeed go to great lengths, but this particular version of it is incapable of proof or disproof, and Perkins' undoubtedly very great influence must surely have exercised itself in a more plausible, if more subtle way. Those, for example who hoarded grain to sell at a higher price in times of scarcity must have been singularly deaf if they fancied Perkins was bolstering common trade practices.[176]

The farthest thing from the minds of these social and religious reformers was the isolation of faith from practice. They believed that faith had every right to advocate its own structure and discipline—even method—on religiously-administered welfare. It was, after all, non-public and religious. For as Alves points out, "social control was still based on principles of charity . . . Thus, poor relief and the reform of personal morals were never far from [their] minds as proper activities for the Christian in the world."[177] About the only difference between Catholic and Protestant welfare at the time was the philosophic difference of approach: whether, with Calvin, the secular world was to be converted into a godly kingdom, or, with Catholicism, that a disciplined religious order should be the body of Christ in the secular world.

Vives, Calvin, Luther, Bucer, and Knox coalesced to form a sur-prisingly consensual approach to the church's role in social wel-fare. They gave great credence to the metaphor of the body being organically related (1 Cor. 12), both poor and non-poor. They reasoned, "Just as injury to the extremities can eventually harm the entire organism, so too prolonged hardship among the poor can feed the flames of civil disorder. When ignored, the poor

---

[176] Ibid., 127.
[177] Alves, op. cit., 15.

generally rise up to demand satisfaction of their needs. Thus, *On the Help of the Poor* portrays relief for the poor as an important tool for the maintenance of social order and control, but it is also presented as a Christian duty with antecedents in classical thought."[178]

For the reformers of nearly five centuries ago, "The moral and spiritual health of the community was thus linked to such practical material concerns as poor relief. For Vives, Calvin, and Loyola, the obsession with the social organism myth and practical poor relief was not accidental."[179] These welfare reformers looked to the past, specifically the canon of Scripture to find the broad principles of social welfare. True, they did not expect that every issue would be addressed by Scripture, but they did expect and did find the broad brushstrokes necessary for erecting a consistent and distinct biblical approach to welfare. The Christian religion, then, established the most powerful and longest lasting welfare model of any in modern western civilization. Only conceit or bias would fail to consult this eminently successful model to glean its enduring principles for our own time.[180]

Are we so sure that it has been empirically demonstrated that poverty cannot benefit from a revival of the diaconate? Can't the Church's ministry help and serve?

R. C. Sproul, Jr., argues that the church may actually be capable of doing mercy better than the Big Federal Government. To the tune of John Lennon's *Imagine*, he commends:

> Imagine all the widows,
> All the orphans too.
> Cared for by families.
> And in the churches too.
> Imagine all the pagans
> Seeing our light shine...

---

[178] Ibid., 7.

[179] Idem.

[180] Cf. My "Early Prototypes of Welfare Reform: The Reformation," in David W. Hall, *The Arrogance of the Modern: Historical Theology Held in Contempt* (Oak Ridge, TN: The Covenant Foundation, 1997), 181-201.

Some may say I'm a dreamer
That things will never change.
But perhaps one day we'll show them
Though now it sounds so strange.

Imagine there's no welfare,
It's easy if you try. . . .
                    Use of Political Categories in the NT

Rather than eschewing political variables, the New Testament actually invokes many political concepts. "Governments" is listed as a charismatic gift (Rom. 12:8; 1 Cor. 12:8) and the Apostle urges for sin not to be allowed to "reign" (Rom. 6:12). The New Testament word for church, *ekklesia,* itself doubles as the term for the meeting of the citizen assembly (Acts 19:23). One early church theologian, Origen, even seems to draw a conscious parallel between the *ekklesia* of God in Athens and Corinth and the civil *ekklesia* is those same municipalities.[181] Besides the frequent reference to "kingdom" in the Gospels and Epistles, Jesus also spoke of an important ecclesiological function in governmental terms: He gave the keys of the KINGDOM (Mt. 16:19). If political categories such as these were inherently evil, our Lord would not have used them as pervasive metaphors.

The chief token of monarchy, the throne, is frequently referenced in the New Testament. At his birth, the angel announced that Jesus will receive the throne of his father David, "and he will reign over the house of Jacob forever; his kingdom will never end" (Lk. 1:33). Jesus did not shrink from speaking of heaven as God's throne (Mt. 5:34), and predicted that the Messiah would sit on a glorious throne (Mt. 19:28). Jesus spoke of his Father as sitting on a throne (Mt.

---

[181] For this reference, I am indebted to Ruben Alvarado's "Church, Kingdom, Liturgy: The Political Language of the New Testament," *Contra Mundum,* No. 12, Summer 1994, 4. Alvarado cites Origen: "And if he who hears this be a candid man, and one who investigates things with a desire to ascertain the truth, he will be filled with admiration of him who not only conceived the design, but also was able to secure in all places the establishment of *ekklesiai* of God alongside of the *ekklesiai* of the people in each city."

23:22), and foretold a time in which he himself would "sit on his throne in heavenly glory" surrounded by all the nations (Mt. 25:31). He also promised his disciples in conjunction with the Sacrament that they would "eat and drink at his table in this kingdom and sit on thrones, judging the twelve tribes of Israel" (Lk. 22:30). David's throne is the proper inheritance of Jesus, according to Acts 2:30; and the Most High has heaven as his throne and the earth as his footstool (Acts 7:49). Colossians 1:16 reveals that Jesus, the co-Creator, is responsible for all "thrones or powers or rulers or authorities." Monarchy *per se* is difficult to dismiss as inherently evil in light of the New Testament usage of such categories, especially when God is addressed as the "King, eternal, immortal, and invisible" (1 Tim. 1:17). Does this not place a limit on our expectations for democracy—even the best—as a panacea for other nations?

Chapter 4

Is Civil Government Absolute?
And Should Christians work for reform?

Theodore Beza: The Point Guard of the American Revolution

To speak to the challenging question of "is it ever right to resist the existing authorities or should Christians be political pacifist, always accepting the status quo?", I wish to call to the witness stand one of the most important thinkers for the American revolution, who is also one of the least known key-players in history. This is also a question that should be asked by those who distrust the status quo. Theodore Beza (1520-1605) was John Calvin's 'Timothy.' He is also like an unnoticed point guard, who commands a basketball team even if he is not the high scorer.

Beza (and Calvin) initially accepted several political notions that were treated as sacred cows. Later, they made unrivalled contributions by questioning the conventional wisdom of the day.[182]

One such sacred cow, based on an improper interpretation of Romans 13, advised that citizens should always, without any exceptions, obey the civil government. Just prior to Luther's ascension—note, and many other Anglican royalist clergy only perpetuated this—immediately prior to the Protestant Reformation, the consensus of Christian political theory held that the Christian citizen had a universal obligation to submit to the civil ruler. Even moral corruption and incompetence were insufficient reasons to revolt against the ruler. Specific governors were viewed as established by divine providence. Prior to Calvin's disciples, the early-sixteenth-century consensus held the following: "[G]overnment *per se* is divinely ordained by God in the Scriptures; bad rulers were sent by God to chastise the nation for their sins; rebellion causes more harm to innocents than to the guilty."[183] William Tyndale stated:

> God hath made the king in every realm judge over all, and over him there is no judge. He that judgeth the king judgeth God, and he that layeth hand on the king layeth hand on God. . . . If the subjects sin, they must be brought to the king's judgement. If the king sins, he must be reserved unto the judgement, wrath and vengeance of God.[184]

Two major lynchpins of political thought, however, changed after Calvin, Beza, and Knox: (a) submission was limited and (b) representation was absolute; these began to be publicized from pulpits and academies. Moreover, only the Protestant religion provided support for these.

The evolution was real, it was philosophically significant, it was politically revolutionary, and it would last for centuries, providing a true turning point in history. Whether one agrees with the hermeneutic or not, the subsequent altered terrain is clear.

---

[182] For more on the importance of Beza, see my *The Genevan Reformation and the American Founding* (Lanham, MD: Lexington Books, 2003).

[183] Keith L. Griffin, *Revolution and Religion: American Revolutionary War and the Reformed Clergy* (New York: Paragon House, 1994), 3.

[184] Keith L. Griffin, *Revolution and Religion*, 3.

The Protestant Reformers, with Calvin at leading the column,[185] thus reformed the exegesis of political texts and did so on valid exegetical grounds. Their new conclusions were superior and caught the attention of the New World, particularly through the Genevan Bible and scholia from the likes of Beza. Theodore Beza's contribution deserves a little more attention.

Beza's two primary works on political matters were his 1554 *Concerning the Punishment of Heretics by the Civil Magistrate* and his 1574 *The Rights of Magistrates*.[186] He was also widely published as a bible commentator and was an early textual critic. Wherever the Huguenots emigrated, they bore Beza's strong Calvinism in their hearts as well as in their enterprise.[187] Shaped by the horrific massacre on St. Bartholomew's Day, this Bezan Calvinism would blaze a trail of resistance to tyrants. At the same time, it frequently expressed its political theory in the language of Scripture, so esteemed in its day. Before Americans adopted Beza's themes, however, Europeans beyond Geneva would extend and adapt his teachings.

Two years after the genocidal Massacre of the Huguenots (and 10 years after Calvin's death), Beza's *The Right of Magistrates* (1574) justified armed resistance against a king if led by intermediating magistrates. The 1572 *St. Bartholomewsnacht* was a turning point in the development of Western political thought and a summons for Calvinism to develop greater application than it had hitherto pioneered. [188] After hearing of the brutal slaughter of the St.

---

[185] For short works that contain biographical sketches of Calvin and a treatise on his managerial skill see my: *The Legacy of John Calvin: His Influence on the Modern World* (Phillipsburg, NJ: Presbyterian and Reformed Publishing, 2008) and *A Heart Promptly Offered: The Revolutionary Leadership of John Calvin* (Nashville, TN: Cumberland House, 2006).

[186] An abridgement of this 1572 work was published in Julian Franklin's *Constitutionalism and Resistance in the Sixteenth Century.* See also my *Calvin in the Public Square: Liberal Democracies, Rights, and Civil Liberties* (Phillipsburg, NJ: Presbyterian and Reformed Publishing, 2009).

[187] For a survey of other Huguenot political tracts, see Quentin Skinner, *The Foundations of Modern Political Thought: The Age of Reformation*, vol. 2 (Cambridge: Cambridge University Press, 1978), 303-307.

[188] Harold Laski avers that this massacre was the critical turning point in

Bartholomew's Day Massacre,[189] Beza, to degrees that Calvin never faced, was forced both to reconsider and also to refine the Calvinist doctrine of political resistance.[190]

Luring many Huguenot leaders to Paris for a wedding in August of 1572, France's Charles IX and Catherine de Medici initiated a gory massacre that began at 2:00 AM on Sunday, August 24th. In the first three days alone, according to John Foxe (who sought refuge in Basle), rampaging marauders killed over 10,000 people in Paris, their Protestant faith serving as the only indictment.[191] Besides Paris, terrified Protestants throughout France sustained the death tolls below:

- 2,000 in Poitiers[192] in one day
- 1,000 at Orleans
- 800 at Lyon (300 in the archbishop's house)
- 500 at Rouen
- 264 at Boutdeauz
- 200 at Toulouse
- 100 at Main.[193]

Calvinistic thought; See Junius Brutus, *A Defense of Liberty Against Tyrants*, trans. Harold J. Laski (Gloucester, MA: Peter Smith, 1963), 10-18.

[189] This 1572 effort to purge Protestants from France eventually resulted in the Edict of Nantes in 1598.

[190] E. William Monter, *Calvin's Geneva* (New York: John Wiley & Sons, 1967), 210. McGrath among others also identifies this massacre as the transformation point. See Alister McGrath, *A Life of John Calvin* (Cambridge, MA: Basil Blackwell Ltd., 1990), 187.

[191] John Foxe, *Foxe's Book of Martyrs*, Marie Gentert King, ed. (Old Tappan, NJ: Spire Books, 1978), 83.

[192] Of interest, many of these cities were the exact locales where Geneva sent missionaries between 1564 and 1572. See Robert M. Kingdon, *Geneva and the Consolidation of the French Protestant Movement, 1564-1572* (Madison, WI: University of Wisconsin Press, 1967), 203-208.

[193] John Foxe, *Foxe's Book of Martyrs*, Marie Gentert King, ed. (Old Tappan, NJ: Spire Books, 1978), 84. In one locale, Augustobona, all Protestants were killed. *Christian History*, Issue 71 (vol. xx, no 3) includes numerous articles on the massacre, leading figues from the French Reformation (including a short essay on Viret), and other helpful information on the subject.

The cold-blooded murder of 60,000 French Huguenots[194] in a single month forced infant Calvinism to face the horror and, now, the inescapable menace of the very depravity that Calvin's writings had been implying. So if Beza extended the logic of Calvin's thought farther than Calvin himself had, he was warranted in moving ahead with a more consistent version of resistance theory. Calvin had begun this shift after the early tensions in France (exhibited in his 1561 Commentary on Daniel), but the devastation and cruelty a decade later unquestionably justified and prodded the thoughts of Beza and others.

Beza came to realize, after Calvin's death, that *absolute submission to a governor*, especially if that governor tyrannically slaughtered thousands, was not divinely sanctioned. Instead, he and others began to complete Calvin's earlier tenets (which Ponet, Viret, and Goodman had already begun before Calvin's death). And one result was that civil governors now had to be seen as deserving only qualified submission—and that on exegetical grounds. Their authority, in other words, was and must be limited.

Beza limited the power of government; a ruler's power was neither infinite nor unconditional. If the ruler was a tyrant, then resistance may be allowed. And in cases of such oppression, the intermediating magistrates were "duty-bound to repress these tyrants who act wildly and commit outrages. If they do not do so, then they shall answer for their disloyalty before the Lord, as traitors to their own country." [195] For Beza, such overthrow was never to be violent

---

[194] Francois Hotman himself stated that the death toll was 50,000. See Donald R. Kelley, *Francois Hotman: A Revolutionary's Ordeal* (Princeton: Princeton University Press, 1973), 219. Another contemporary, John Foxe cited similar numbers. See John Foxe, *Foxe's Book of Martyrs*, Marie Gentert King, ed., (Old Tappan, NJ: Spire Books, 1978), 83-84. Later, Jonathan Edwards set the level of disaster even higher, noting that within one generation France lost 39 princes, 148 counts, 234 barons, 147,518 gentlemen, and 760,000 common people to genocidal persecution. Cited in William M. Cox, "The Standards and Civil Government," *Memorial Volume of the Westminster Assembly, 1647-1897* (Richmond, VA: Presbyterian Committee of Publication, 1897), 287. See also Robert M. Kingdon, *Geneva and the Consolidation of the French Protestant Movement, 1564-1572* (Madison, WI: University of Wisconsin Press, 1967).

[195] Citations to this work by Beza in this section are taken from Patrick Poole's

("the rule is steadfast and perpetual"). Beza reminded his audience that, whenever they could not obey the commands of rulers without "offending the majesty and despising the authority of the King of kings and the Lord of lords," then they must not participate in revolution. A believer must obey God above all and not acquiesce to government-ordered ill behavior under the guise of civic obedience. This was a striking advance in political theory that shaped the modern world.

Beza, like Calvin before him, balanced these sentiments by noting that *private* citizens were not to overthrow the magistrate, even if the rulers were tyrants, "for that is a far different thing from refusing to yield obedience unto impious or unjust laws [edicts]." In addition, he called on Christians to avoid contentiousness, while not forfeiting the right to defend themselves against a tyrant. He wrote that those who suggested that it was unlawful for Christians to seek and maintain their rights by civil pleas were deceived. He concluded: "As often as the Magistrate commands anything that is repugnant either to the worship which we owe unto God, or to the love which we owe unto our neighbor, we cannot yield obedience thereunto with a safe conscience. For as often as the commandment of God and men are directly opposed one against another, this rule is to be perpetually observed; that it is better to obey GOD than men."[196]

Others went so far as to urge that in these cases, overthrow was mandatory.[197] Of course, most of these views, as in the case of

---

edition (and may thus be searched electronically), posted at: http://www.constitution.org/cmt/beza/magistrates.htm. Modern editions of this work are Karl Sturm, ed., *De Iure Magistratuum* (Neukirchen, 1965), and Robert M. Kingdon, ed., *De Droit des magistrats* (Geneva, 1971).

[196] Theodore Beza, *The Grounds and Principles of Christian Religion*, 262.

[197] Beza qualified the duty to rebel against the civil magistrate, restricting such duty by the following notions: (1) "no one in private station is allowed to set himself in open violence against a tyrant" (Question 6); (2) "that the tyranny must be undisguised and notorious;" (3) "that the recourse should not be had to arms before all other remedies have been tried;" and (4) "Nor yet before the question has been thoroughly examined, not only as to what is permissible, but also as to what is expedient, lest the remedies prove more hazardous than the very disease." (Question 7). See Theodore Beza, *Concerning the Rights of Rulers over Their Subjects and the Duty of Subjects Towards Their Rulers*, Henry-Louis Gonin,

Scotland and England, depended on the notion that God had established a religious covenant with a nation, which implied a continuing corporate responsibility to a previous covenant.

If one senses progress in thought on the topic of restraining government by comparing this work with Calvin's earliest discussions, the likely explanation for the development resides in the reaction to the St. Bartholomew's Day massacre. This stunning slaughter (which today might be called genocide) virtually extinguished a local politico-religious movement—French Protestant churches had grown from zero to 2,150[198] in the generation prior to 1572—forcing Calvinists like Beza (who had close contacts and interaction with the French churches) to extend the logic of their principles even further.[199] In addition, the exegesis of key texts (e.g., the household tables in the epistles, Acts 4-5, and Romans 13) was expanded to account for such dawning realizations. The resulting evolution rapidly moved from the possibility of lawful resistance to the moral obligation to oppose evil rulers.

This massacre was both the coming of age and a fault point for Calvinistic political theory. While Calvin was alive, he and Beza had discouraged rebellion and recommended support of existing rulers if at all possible. However, with the treacherous slaughter and virtual extinction of Reformed religion in France, Beza led efforts to reassess the theory. In so doing, he proved that modifications within limits not only did not harm the theoretical

---

trans. (Pretoria, South Africa: H. A. U. M., 1956); also posted at: http://www.constitution.org/cmt/beza/magistrates.htm.

[198] Although some of the churches were no doubt small, the existence of 1,785 Consistories in France by 1562 reveals the magnitude of this Huguenot explosion. Alister McGrath, *A Life of John Calvin* (Cambridge, MA: Basil Blackwell Ltd., 1990), 184. The 1852 edition of Calvin's Commentary on Daniel claims that Beza had up to 40,000 followers near Paris, that each of the 2,150 churches had its own pastor, and that the Huguenots were nearly one-third as numerous as the Catholic population.

[199] Earlier, an abridgement of Beza's *Concerning the Rights of Rulers Over Their Subjects and The Duty Of Subjects Towards Their Rulers* was available in Julian H. Franklin, ed. *Constitutionalism and Resistance in the Sixteenth Century* (New York: Pegasus, 1969).

foundations of Calvinism but rather actually improved its effectiveness. The result was that what once appeared radical (the suggestions of Knox, Vermigli, and Ponet) would become the norm for Calvinists. Beza thus transformed Calvinism and normalized resistance to evil governments on biblical bases.

These developments went beyond the situations that Calvin had faced; and it is a tribute to Calvin's mentoring that Beza so ably addressed these life-and-death challenges. The resistance theory that grew out of this tragedy is a tribute to the adaptability of Calvin's thought. In Beza's case, after serving so faithfully as Calvin's understudy, when a crisis arose he responded to tragedy by proposing better measures—ones that were consistent with the character of Calvinism.

Of course, much of Beza's diplomatic career stemmed from Calvin's own efforts in this area. Few modern theologians have had the amount of political involvement that Calvin had. He consistently received briefings on affairs of state, regularly corresponded with officials at the highest levels, and tirelessly watched for opportunities to spread his political gospel.[200] Indicative of his correspondence, he dedicated his commentary on the Catholic Epistles to King Edward VI of England, his commentary on Isaiah to Queen Elizabeth, and his commentary on Hebrews to King Sigismund of Poland. Some of his former students even briefed him on political developments after they left Geneva, and Calvin's advice would extend throughout European Christendom. Calvin sought to provoke political change through his writings rather than through social upheaval. He pled in a letter on October 1, 1560: "I never approved of deciding our cause by violence and arms."[201] The result, as one non-Protestant scholar put it, is that "in the political domain, Calvinist ideas are at the origin of the revolution which from the eighteenth to the nineteenth

---

[200] J. T. McNeill, "John Calvin on Civil Government," *Calvinism and the Political Order*, George L. Hunt, ed. (Philadelphia: Westminster Press, 1965), 24.

[201] Cited in J. T. McNeill, "John Calvin on Civil Government," *Calvinism and the Political Order*, George L. Hunt, ed., 24.

centuries gave birth and growth to the parliamentary democracies of Anglo-Saxon type."[202] Beza would continue that political theology of action until his own death in 1605. History would find that his groundbreaking and courageous questioning of the status quo of political thought for his day would assist the spread of republics, the deposition of tyrants, and the clergy who so strongly supported the American revolution.

To this day, wherever there is tyranny or oppression, people who acquaint themselves with Beza and his political Calvinism find a friend of liberty. Such began by calling into question pre-existing political dogmas—and examining those in light of the whole of revelation.

The Question of Limits on Submission: Is it absolute?

In what instances is resistance to authority permissible? And how do we express dissent? The vast majority of New Testament (and Old Testament) teaching calls upon Christians to submit to and support the governing authorities. Indeed, some believe that there are no exceptions to the commands (Romans 13; 1 Peter 2) that summon submission to the governing authorities. However, the larger stream of orthodox interpretation has acknowledged that in some rare cases, resistance to the civil authorities is justified. The basis for this is found in certain instances in the Scripture. For example, Daniel did not obey the king when he was ordered to eat certain foods. He sought and received an exemption. Technically, he was still within the law. However, when it came to the king prohibiting his prayer, then Daniel did not obey that injunction. Christian ethics has no disagreement with his activity. Likewise, the Israelite midwives disobeyed Pharaoh's order to kill the Hebrew males when they were delivered. They, too, were justified.

The principle which allows for such resistance to authority is that if an earthly power is in unavoidable conflict with divine prerogatives, then Christians must obey God as a more basic duty

---

[202] Cited by Paul T. Fuhrmann, "Philip Mornay and the Huguenot Challenge to Absolutism," *Calvinism and the Political Order*, George L. Hunt, ed., 50.

than obeying earthly politicians. When the Lord commanded believers to love God above all others and serve only God—making no idols, nor giving no higher allegiances—the seeds of a principle of proper resistance were sown. When Jesus agreed by stating that "no one can serve two Masters (Mt. 6:24), the potential conflict of loyalties was validated. If in conflict, then one must never elevate the earthly magistrate above the divine Sovereign. In some cases when an earthly ruler becomes evil and arrogant, in practice usurping the exclusive prerogatives of God, he must be resisted; lest God is dishonored.

Several examples occur in the Book of Acts. Other than Paul's appeal to Caesar, the only New Testament instances of overt resistance to authority that are countenanced are in Acts 4-5. Some have seen these as inconsistent with the other predominant teachings in the NT. A better way to see these is not as inconsistencies but as situations that comport with the other normal rules, yet with an important difference. While the New Testament does not normally advocate political rebellion, neither does it commit the believer to an absolute obedience to earthly rulers who contradict other revelations of God. In the explanation below, an attempt is made to honor the commands to submit to civil authorities, the exceptions to that rule being clearly noted.

Such exceptions to the rule can be formulated as criteria for resistance. Similar to the traditional "Just War" theory with its criteria that are formulated, it is helpful if we have a short list of criteria which demarcate permissible resistance.

The first thing to note about the passages (Acts 4-5) is that the resistance was not primarily against civil authorities. This oft-overlooked fact has significant, if not compelling, force. Peter and John had been arrested by the Sanhedrin for proclaiming the gospel. To cease such would be in direct violation to explicit commands by Jesus to spread the Word (Mt. 28:18). The authorities thus forced a show-down, claiming obedience which would have coerced sin on the part of Christians. Peter and John necessarily disobeyed. Yet, it is significant that their disobedience is not against the civil rulers, the Romans. It is against ecclesiastical authority that they affirm:

"Judge for yourselves whether it is right in God's sight to obey you rather than God. For we cannot help speaking about what we have seen and heard" (Acts 4:19-20).

Even if that distinction is not absorbed, nonetheless, several sufficient criteria or pre-conditions for resistance are provided here. *First*, it is not unlawful to resist an ecclesiastical body if it insists on error. *Second*, the accusation against these disciples was the allegation that they were violating a speech code; they were simply preaching. Hence, it may be acceptable to resist by oral or written disagreement. Indeed, these methods should be tried first. *Third*, they resisted obeying the authorities because it was impossible to do otherwise: "We cannot help . . ." (Acts 4:20). To obey the authorities would have been to sin.

A key difference should be noted at this juncture. It is one thing for a government to permit activities which a Christian believes to be unethical. For example, if a state allows prostitution, abortion, or the use of drugs, but does not compel the Christian to participate in any of those, then it is possible for the Christian to simply avoid such. There is a material difference between a state which allows prostitution or abortion, however, as opposed to one that mandates either. In cases where laws permit, but do not coerce to sin, the Christian need not forcibly rebel. Abstinence from the sin along with patient attempts to inculcate better morality and legislation are called for in that case. Yet, those are very different from a case in which Christians are forbidden to evangelize or are arrested if they believe in Christ. In those cases, believers have no choice but to resist, to disobey, and to face whatever punishment results. Not to do so is to sin. Hence, the third pre-condition which justifies resistance is that the state must positively enforce a citizen's committing of sin. In those cases, believers are not only justified in resisting, but expected to resist.

Fourth, early Christians were willing to accept punishment, and at times did. The action must not be immune from lawful punishment. *Fifth*, their resistance was not violent nor destructive of property. And *sixth*, this resistance was over a matter of real substance; not something trivial.

Six questions one must answer prior to justifying resistance are:
* 1. Is it a matter of enduring principal, or a matter of comfort, tradition, or expedience? If the latter, then resistance is not justified. Christians are called on to suffer minor inconveniences (1 Cor. 4:12; 1 Pet. 2:13-18).
* 2. Is the resistance violent and destructive, or is it peaceful? Even grave hostilities do not automatically justify resistance.
* 3. Is the Christian willing to accept the lawful punishment? If not, then resistance should not be undertaken.
* 4. Is some act positively enjoined by the government—with power to punish—or does the government show its ungodliness by allowing more immorality than the code of God's Kingdom? If possible to do otherwise (Is it avoidable?), then the Christian should exhibit personal righteousness and not partake of immoral practices. The mere existence of immoral practices without civil punishment does not legitimate rebellion.
* 5. Is it a matter that can be kept to oneself, and internally believed with integrity? If possible, Christians are to be at peace with all people, even at times keeping their opinions to ourselves. The First Amendment to the U.S. Constitution grants freedom of speech and the press. While agreeing with these values, they are nowhere set down as scriptural rights.
* 6. Is the resistance against the lawful civil authority or some other? To qualify as civil resistance, it must be against formal secular powers—not so much against ecclesiastical, traditional, corporate, or other powers.[203]

These can be further illustrated in Acts 5. Again the disciples were arrested (Acts 5:18; note, the notion of incarceration is not condemned by this passage). They had been flogged, and are now arrested again. Yet, miraculously, an angel released them. They are summoned to the Sanhedrin again (Acts 5:27). They are upbraided for continuing their public proclamation. In answer to this, Peter

---

[203] We could also add a few others: Calls for submission to a national government do not apply to international situations, as if to imply either submission to foreign states, nor pacifism in general. The *seventh* criteria might be: Is it resistance against one's own country? or some international confederation?

replied, "We must obey God rather than men" (Acts 5:30). This was not reached lightly, but there was an unavoidable conflict. Thus, the believers had to obey God rather than impostors to sovereignty.

These six pre-conditions are helpful and help provide consistency to biblical teaching. They refine the rule as calling for the norm of submission but illustrate the criteria when the rule may not apply. They also show how other alleged biblical cases of "rebellion" were acceptable. The Hebrew midwives met the conditions above. When ordered to maintain a certain diet, Daniel negotiated with the rulers, for not all of these criteria were present. However, when he was ordered not to pray, with the above criteria satisfied, he was justified in resistance. The same is true for a modern instance, such as Corrie ten Boom's hiding of Jews during WWII. When these pre-conditions are met—analogous to a "Just War"—there is "Just Resistance."

Dabney also mimed the reformation maxim that, "an unjust government is far better than none at all. It . . . should be obeyed by individuals, rather than have anarchy."[204] On the subject of resistance, the Chaplain to General Stonewall Jackson noted, "If the thing commanded by the civil magistrate is positively sinful, then the Christian citizen must refuse obedience, but yield submission to the penalty therefore."[205] While arguing against indefinite passive obedience to an evil form of government, he also remarked: "God has not ordained what government mankind shall live under, but only that they shall live under a government. . . . When a form of government entirely ceases, as a whole, to subserve its proper end, is it still to subsist forever? This is preposterous. . . . The meaning of the apostle is, that this resistance must be the act, not of the individual, but of the people. The insubordination which he condemns, is that which arrays against a bad government . . . the worse anarchy of the individual will."[206]

---

[204] Robert L. Dabney, *Lectures in Systematic Theology* (rpr. Grand Rapids: Baker, 1985), 870.
[205] Idem.
[206] Ibid., 872.

What about Appeals?

Is it legitimate to resort to judicial procedures? Imprisonment for crimes is accepted by the NT. Nevertheless, there are cases in which judicial bodies make mistakes. When they do, an appeal is in order. The Book of Acts records an extended and notorious case of a Christian exercising his civil right to an appeal. When the apostle Paul was arrested, he did not passively acquiesce to those who had improperly arrested him. He resisted, but resisted in a lawfully-established fashion, availing himself to the Roman legal system and its civic protections. No censure of this ever appearing in Scripture, it is generally accepted that such appeals are countenanced by God.

In Paul's case, his appeal was not based on some foundation provided directly by God. Rather, as a Roman citizen Paul had rights to appeal his case all the way to Caesar. When lawful appeals are constitutional, a Christian does not sin by availing himself to those. When Paul was first imprisoned, he was released by a miraculous earthquake (Acts 16:26). He did not immediately escape, but evangelized the jailer who would have resorted to suicide. The suicide prevented, Paul baptized the jailer (never calling for him to resign this particular occupation) and his household (Acts 16:34). The next day, when these events are unfolded, the city leaders wish to quietly release Paul and Silas who, however, claim that they are "Roman" citizens (Acts 16:37). One of the fundamental rights as a Roman citizen was a right to a fair and public trial. When this right was trampled, Paul did not hesitate to invoke it (16:38) to the chagrin of the magistrates. Upon learning this, these magistrates seek appeasement (16:39). Lacking other scriptural prohibition, it is not wrong to avail oneself to lawful judicial procedures.

Paul's appeal to Caesar is widely known. When he was arrested at Jerusalem, he identified himself as a Jew, but also as a "citizen," (Acts 21:39) and later clarified that he was a Roman citizen (Acts 22:25). As he does so, the law enforcers cease their punishment and allow him the right of appeal. Insofar as his disagreement with the Jews was a religious matter (Acts 24:12, 21) that was not under the purview of civil law, Paul pursued his appeal. Several higher magistrates found him innocent (Acts 26:31-32), but still allowed his appeal to Caesar. As he arrived in Rome (Acts 28:19), he reviewed the necessity for appeal to Caesar. Paul remained under house arrest for 2 years and was likely released due to lack of evidence. In the interim, he was used mightily to evangelize many in the upper echelons of the Roman government (Phil. 1:13). Lawful appeals are not instances of sinful resistance to authority.[207]

Belief among the ruling class: As Paul concludes his Epistle to the Romans, chapter 16 speaks of several Romans of high standing who had become Christians. One of those was "Erastus, the city's director of public works" (Rom. 16:23). Apparently, a Roman could become a Christian and still serve in a high position of leadership. These "public works" by inference were permitted as a lawful function of government, else calls for the resignation of Erastus would have been issued. As already noted, the Philippian jailer was not told to resign from his work in the criminal justice system of the day. Later, the impact of the gospel spread to "the whole Praetorian Guard" (Phil. 1:13), who did not resign on the spot but continued to serve in government. The Epistles even speak of a paid military (1 Cor. 9:7) as legitimate. These were permissible functions of the state, and Christian converts could serve in good conscience. In time, Christianity reached many in the ruling classes. The New Testament also bears witness, though, to the fact that not many Christians in the first century were of noble birth, high standing, nor influential status (1 Cor. 1:26-28).

Governance is a charismatic gift: Far from being inherently tainted, the ability to govern is dignified by being listed among the spiritual gifts (Rom. 12:8; 1 Cor. 12:28). It is true that this is primarily a gift for ecclesiological administration, however, civil governors, if animated by that same Spirit may also be uniquely gifted for matters of civil government.

---

[207] Note, this may be the *eighth* criteria to go with the others above: Does resistance use a lawful method? The *ninth* criteria raises the question: Does resistance use other intermediaries, e.g., the lesser magistrates?

Method: As believers labor in political matters, they are tempted to employ the political methods of those who may not share their faith and ethic. Accordingly, the New Testament mandates that Christian political involvement is to be executed with a different *ethos*: "For though we live in the world, we do not wage war as the world does. The weapons we fight with are not the weapons of the world" (2 Cor. 10:3-4). More effective than the world's armamentarium is the one given to the Christian who must take care not to lapse into an "ends justifies the means" mentality. There are certain methods (e. g., theft, slander, immorality) which must be avoided by the Christian statesman, even if unpopularity or defeat ensues. Tactical decisions by involved Christians must be legislated by the norms of Christ, as are the ends of political involvement.

Citizenship: Citizenship appears to be a lawful New Testament concept. Used by the Apostle Paul on several occasions, it is a beneficial category for the state. Gentile believers were at one time "excluded from citizenship in Israel" (Eph. 2:12). However, all believers are granted citizenship status in God's *oikonomia* (Eph. 2:19) and are no longer considered aliens to that spiritual entity. The most important status is to have one's citizenship in heaven (Phil. 3:20), which citizenship transcends any earthly national or party loyalty.

Lawful Court System: Paul spoke of lawful courts and was the recipient of a favorable judicial appeal. Moreover, the New Testament also addresses the need for church discipline which was carried out by ecclesiological judiciaries (1 Cor. 5). As to lawsuits among fellow-believers, a judicial system of lawful courts is assumed and regulated by the norm of fellowship in the NT. Believers are not to degenerate to the level of hostility that requires civil justice resolution.[208] They may even suffer loss (1 Cor. 6:7) or be wronged, but their disputes are to be adjudicated by church

---

[208] Bruce Winter, *Seek the Welfare of the City* (Grand Rapids: Eerdmans, 1994), 107-118 provides a current analysis of civic litigation in the first century.

courts, if necessary. Thus, both ecclesiological courts and civil courts are warranted and necessary as legitimate functions of government. Without either, unrest will grow and become destructive. Civil courts are preferable to judicial anarchy. Ecclesiological courts are to proceed in fairness, with measured sentences ranging from verbal rebuke to declaratory condemnation (Gal. 1:8) to excommunication (1 Cor. 5:5) if necessary. But the two court systems should not be intermingled, as both Scripture and history teach.

Law: The Christian view of law is, in general, a positive one. Far from despising the law, the New Testament teaches that God's law is good, spiritual and positive (Rom. 7:12; 1 Tim. 1:8-11). Jesus and others consistently support the law; they do not overturn it (Mt. 5:18-19). Paul states that, "the law is good if one uses it properly . . . law is made not for the righteous but for law-breakers" (1 Tim. 1:8-9). Agreeing with the Psalmist that the law of God is of great and enduring value (Ps. 19:6-8), the New Testament consistently encourages respect for the civil law, as well as for divine law. Christians are not above the law, but view it positively as a pedagogue (Gal. 3:24-25). The law has utility to restrain from evil (*usus politicus*), to teach God's standards (*usus didactcus*), and to convict humans of their sinful imperfection (*usus convictus*).

Yet it is also important to understand that the law has a "lawful" use. If put to illegitimate uses, the law may not be effective. For example, Paul teaches that the law's purpose was to provide an objective moral measurement (Gal. 3:19) but is not opposed to God's working by grace (Gal. 3:21). The law cannot, however, "impart life" or give righteousness (Gal. 3:22). It is an external regulator and should not be confused with a mechanism which in and of itself creates righteousness. Law and grace are not opposed in the economy of God, but neither are they equivalent. Both must function in their assigned areas.

Christians will respect the rule of law in society. At times, they will even be called upon to be subject to administrations which are less than righteous.

Subjection to Unrighteous Governors: Christians may well endure persecution (1 Cor. 4:12). If in God's providence that occurs, Christians are not mandated to cause a revolution, although certain conditions may warrant one. The predominant New Testament response to evil governments is subjection. Paul instructs Titus to remind his church "to be subject to rulers and authorities, to be obedient, to be ready to do whatever is good, to slander no one [including the ruler], to be peaceable and considerate, and to show true humility toward all men" (Tit. 3:1-2). These civic duties do not call for non-subjection. Later, the Book of Hebrews instructs: "Obey your leaders and submit to their authority. They keep watch over you as men who must give an account. Obey them so that their work will be a joy, not a burden" (Heb. 13:17). It is likely that the primary reference of that command is to church elders; however, the principle of subjection for witness carries over into the civil realm.

Commenting on 1 Timothy 2, John Calvin explained:

He [Paul] expressly mentions kings and other magistrates, because more than all others they might be hated by Christians. All the magistrates who existed at that time were so many sworn enemies of Christ; and therefore this thought might occur to them, that they ought not to pray for those who devoted all their power and all their wealth to fight against the kingdom of Christ . . . The apostle meets this difficulty, and expressly enjoins Christians to pray for them also. And, indeed, the depravity of men is not a reason why God's ordinance should not be loved. . . . seeing that God appointed magistrates and princes for the preservation of mankind, however much they fall short of the divine appointment, still we must not on that account cease to love what belongs to God, and to desire that it may remain in force. . . . The universal doctrine is this, that we should desire the continuance and peaceful condition of those governments which have been appointed by God.[209]

---

[209] John Calvin, *Commentary on I Timothy* (Grand Rapids: Baker Bookhouse, 1979), vol. xxi, 51.

Peter provides a lengthy treatise on the value and necessity of submission to civil rulers. He makes it clear that the believer is to submit "for the Lord's sake to every authority instituted among men." It is the manifest providence of God—in whatever governmental form—to which Christians are to submit. Peter clarifies that no particular form of government has ultimate priority in human affairs and that Christians are to apply this command equally for subjection, regardless of the form of government in the state: "Whether to the king as supreme authority [monarchy] to governors sent by him [delegated representatives]" (1 Pet. 2:14), Christians are to be obedient unless the sufficient conditions for resistance are present. Christians were also summoned to live public lives which "enhanced the life of the cities in which they lived."[210]

In this important Petrine passage, the two most categorical functions of government are defined: "to punish those who do wrong and to commend those who do right" (1 Pet. 2:14). The state is to maintain standards of law and punish those who harm others by breaking the law. Such legal standards determine "wrong," and criminal punishments are appropriate for the wrong-doers. On the other hand, those who do right are commended by the officers of the state. Such commendation normally takes the form of protection, good-will, peace, and assistance.

Peter promises that evangelistic opportunities occur for those who evidence such matur-ity and perseverance as to maintain godliness even in situations of unfairness. Slaves are used as an example yet again in this passage (1 Pet. 2:18). Christians are called to be more concerned with "doing good" (1 Pet. 2:15) than with receiving all that might otherwise be afforded them civilly. They are

---

[210] Bruce Winter, *Seek the Welfare of the City* (Grand Rapids: Eerdmans, 1994), 1. In his study of Christian Benefaction in the first century, Winter notes that exhortation (like Peter's) was necessary in order to prevent a wholesale withdrawal from a hostile culture. To offset some of the public animus, wealthy Christians were to assume the role of public benefactors: "The New Testament stance is clear—their light was to shine that men would see their good works and glorify their Father in heaven. Furthermore, the rich, be they Christian or non-Christian, would have been expected, either by custom or law, to undertake public office as part of their liturgy." op. cit., 22.

to show respect to everyone, including giving honor to the king (1 Pet. 2:17). A monarchy is thus, neither excluded nor necessarily normed.

What biblical means of resistance are available?

Based on the above review and discussion, the following are permissible means of resistance, beginning in order.

    a. Pray
    b. Flee
    c. Preach (Acts 4-5)
    d. Martyrdom
    e. Appeal to intermediate magistrates
    f. Revolution

Remembering how Calvin and Luther later feared zealotry and embraced moderation and order is a great reminder. There are good reasons for their concerns about mobocracy, then and now.

Help From the Past: Five Points of Political thought from the Reformers

By the early seventeenth century, a new political tradition was congcaling. A summary from a Dartmouth historian Herbert Foster about a century ago noted the following as hallmarks of Calvin's political legacy, and most are exhibited by the works of his closest disciples referenced above:

(1) The absolute sovereignty of God entailed that universal human rights (or Beza's "fundamental law") should be protected and must not be surrendered to the whim of tyranny.
(2) These fundamental laws, which were always compatible with God's law, are the basis of whatever public liberties we enjoy.
(3) Mutual covenants, as taught by Beza, Hotman, and the *Vindiciae*, between rulers and God and between rulers and subjects were binding and necessary.

(4) As Ponet, Knox, and Goodman taught, the sovereignty of the people flows logically from the mutual obligations of the covenants above.
(5) The representatives of the people, not the people themselves, are the first line of defense against tyranny.[211]

I have summarized the five points of political Calvinism slightly differently, referring to:

- Depravity as a perennial human variable to be accommodated;
- Accountability for leaders provided via a *collegium*;
- Republicanism as the preferred form of government;
- Constitutionalism needed to restrain both the rulers and the ruled; and
- Limited government, beginning with the family, as foundational.

The resulting mnemonic device, DARCL (though not as convenient as TULIP), seems a more apt summary if placed in the context of the political writings of Calvin's disciples.[212]

Whether one agrees with all of Calvin's theology or not, the subsequent altered terrain is clear. And Calvin, whether it is in his *Institutes*, or in his commentaries and sermons, stood at the font of a new, or renewed, political tradition.

Moreover, this Calvinistic view of government can provide guidance in matters like the following:

- It may demand more accountability on stimulus grants (like the 2008 TARP grants) to prevent exploitation.
- It gives pause to and holds limited expectations for nation building.

---

[211] *Collected Papers of Herbert D. Foster* (privately printed, 1929), 174. These ideas were reiterated in Beza, Buchanan, Peter Martyr, Althusius, Hotman, Daneau, *Vindiciae*, Ponet, William the Silent, & others.

[212] For my earlier work on this topic, see *Savior or Servant: Putting Government in Its Place* (Oak Ridge, TN: Kuyper Institute, 1996). For a more recent short summary of Calvin's view see my "Calvin on Human Government and the State," in David W. Hall and Peter A. Lillback, eds., *A Theological Guide to Calvin's Institutes: Essays and Analysis* (Phillipsburg, NJ: Presbyterian and Reformed Publishing, 208), 411-439.

- It prioritized the written constitution, not merely the whim of a majority party.
- It consistently leads citizens to have non-utopian expectations for their leaders.
- It also suggests that believers should not only be interested in but also active in matters of local and national politics.

The New Testament frequently speaks of principalities (Col. 1:16), rulers (1 Cor. 2:8; 15:24; Eph. 1:21; Eph. 2:2; Eph. 3:10; Eph. 6:12; Col. 1:16), kings (1 Cor. 4:8), ambassadors (2 Cor. 5:20), authorities (Eph. 1:21; Col. 1:16; 2:15), and dominions (Eph. 1:21; Col. 1:13; Tit. 3:2). These metaphors are no more improper than metaphors for athletics, farming, or other metaphors. The categories themselves are not evil or sub-Christian. Christians are members, political citizens (*politeia*; Eph. 2:19), of the new Israel. Ruben Alvarado concludes his study of New Testament political terminology: "[T]he New Testament's adoption of the language of the *polis* to describe the nature and ministry of the church means that the contemporary privatized view of the church is erroneous. From the beginning the church's ministry has been public, even when it has gone unrecognized. We moderns have accepted the lie that the church is not and cannot be a public institution. But like it or not, that is what she is."[213] The New Testament does not avoid governmental matters; it seeks to transform them and "take every thought captive" to Christ (2 Cor. 10:5).[214]

---

[213] Ibid., 6.

[214] John H. Yoder summarizes the biblical teaching about these powers. He asserts that: (1) They are "in their general essence parts of a good creation"; (2) "But these structures fail to serve us as they should. They do not enable humanity to live a genuinely free, loving life. They have absolutized themselves and they demand from the individual and society an unconditional loyalty. They harm and enslave us." and (3) "We are lost in the world, in its structures, and in the current of its development. But nonetheless it is in this world that we have been preserved . . . Our lostness and our survival are inseparable, both dependent upon the Powers." See his *The Politics of Jesus,* 2nd edition (Grand Rapids: Eerdmans, 1994), 142.

Bruce Winter has summarized the New Testament emphasis on *politeia*: "A survey of the use of *politeuomia* in the political or civic discussions in inscriptions and papyri shows how widespread the meaning of 'to live as citizens' was. What also emerges is that it was aligned with terms from *politeia*. From an investigation of over 250 of its occurrences . . . this word is linked with 'concord' and means functioning in harmony with public life."[215] Christians were expected to transform the *politeia*.

[215] Bruce Winter, *Seek the Welfare of the City* (Grand Rapids: Eerdmans, 1994), 102.

Chapter 5

What is Your Most Important and Lasting Political Contribution?

Understand the Biblical Pattern of Government: A key text

It is said that if table conversation is to remain friendly, it should treat both religion and politics with *detente*. The passage considered in this chapter violates both rules of polite dinner conversation at the same time. In fact, not only does this passage broach those subjects, but furthermore, it puts them in right order. This is one of the more important chapters in all of Scripture for Christians in all times to understand.

The Bible does not explicitly reveal a divine position on all political ideas, bills, and treaties—although biblical principles underpin or contradict most legislation. All legislative measures should have their presuppositions, prudence, and prospects measured by Scripture. As far as explicit counsel from God on some subjects, however, the divine rule has not been revealed for all matters of policy. At times, one has to be satisfied with general principles; all that one might like to know has not been revealed.

Since the Bible does not pretend to issue opinions on every political issue, certain proposals must be evaluated with prudence.

For example, I often answer a practical question with a practical answer. Often Christians ask: Can I vote for an official who does not share my faith or most of my views. Is a vote, a covenant or a preference? I have a number of friends who conscientiously do not wish to vote for a candidate unless he satisfies a large number of their interests and beliefs. To vote for one who is less than orthodox on all theological and ethical variables, some think, is to make an oath or covenant with an ungodly politician. On the other hand, some will vote for a candidate, regardless of numerous ideological or moral failings, primarily because of friendships or benefits promised. One thing that helps is to remember that voting for a political candidate is not the same as voting for an elder or pastor. When we vote in civil elections, we express our preference—often from among flawed candidates—and instead of viewing this as a covenanting ceremony in a ballot booth, it may be more practical and helpful to view this as expressing a preference.

Our concern, however, is not with what God has *not* revealed, but to be faithful to what he *has* revealed. We should be enormously pleased if Christians merely acted on the amount of revealed information in civic affairs. About 3 decades ago, Richard J. Neuhaus wrote about an abysmal abdication from the public sector in *The Naked Public Square*. Perhaps as truthfully as any, he captured our age with that metaphor. His argument was that, whereas once monuments to religious values stood in colonial public squares, now those same secularized public squares have been stripped, leaving monuments naked and devoid of reference to spiritual or eternal values.

Nations have opportunities to reclothe public squares with foundational spiritual values, or else they may trek downward along the path of godlessness, toward further deterioration. Christians need to be armed with the sword of God's Word in reforming the state, not with worldly weapons (2 Cor. 10:4).

With that in mind, there is no clearer single passage to study on God and government than Romans 13. This is the fullest single treatment of that subject in revealed literature. God has not left believers in the dark about matters of state but has addressed those also in his unerring Word. Along with the previous biblical teaching on government, Romans 13 supports and enhances a coherent view of the state. God has created human government to be a blessing for his people; and as long as this government is under God, it will be and should be supported. Rather than "of the people, by the people, and for the people," the scriptural view is that government is "over the people, under God, for his glory, and for the common good" (WCF 23:1).

Christians do well to note some of the features of this passage, along with God's prescriptions for the role of the state. After these matters are understood correctly, then the role of the citizen will be addressed.

Key Assumptions

God has designed government to work, and that necessarily involves authority. Authority is the proper discharge of responsibility by those who are assigned certain tasks. A recent statement of faith surmises: "Human society can be neither well-ordered nor prosperous unless it has some people invested with legitimate authority."[216] The opposite of authority is anarchy—the rule of lawlessness. In a state without authority, society becomes chaotic.

There is a long history of respect for authority among biblical Christians. God's people quickly came to understand that precisely because they were sinful creatures, they needed some order, enforcement, and government. Government will be present in heaven, submitted to the Divine monarch. However, this side of heaven, the need for enforced restraint will persist as long as sinners

---

[216] *Catechism of the Catholic Church* (Liguori, MO: Liguori Publications, 1995), 463.

can have their way. That is true in the three major spheres of God's creation: the state, the church, and the home.

From the outset, God is the one who established authority; and submission to it—far from being demeaning or bad—is a definite good. Authority and governments are God's ideas. As this passage teaches, it is only the rebel who fights against that God-ordained institution. The foundation or basis of the state is rooted nowhere other than in his own plan. The state is not merely a human creation.

Many maintain that orderly government is only the result of a voluntary compact between citizens based on their own good will. However, rooting the basis of the state in the human being or human decision is not the biblical view: "Some have supposed that the right or legitimate authority of human government has its foundation ultimately in 'the consent of the governed,' 'the will of the majority,' or in some imaginary 'social compact' entered into by the fore-fathers of the race at the origin of social life. It is self-evident however, that the divine will is the source of all government; and the obligation to obey that will, resting upon all moral agents, the ultimate ground of all obligation to obey human governments."[217]

It is crucial to see that God is the Creator of government in general, and governments in particular, lest one seek to overturn something which God has instituted. Verse 1 gives the categorical command that everyone (not some, or a few, but all) must submit to the governing authorities. The authorities spoken of here are civil, not so much spiritual.[218] Certainly, other places speak of the need and value of submitting to Godly authorities in the church (e. g., 1 Pet. 5), but the focus here is civil authority.[219]

---

[217] A. A. Hodge, *The Confession of Faith* (Edinburgh: Banner of Truth, 1978), 293.

[218] Oscar Cullmann, *The State in the New Testament* (New York: Charles Scribner's Sons, 1956), 95-114, collects recent comment on *exousia*, in which he argues that "authorities" has a dual reference to both governmental agents and angels. He noted that elsewhere the New Testament uniformly uses this term of angelic powers. However, admitting the context, therefore, he pleads for a dual reference rather than opting for an exclusive reference.

[219] Craig Blomberg, "The Globalization of Biblical Hermeneutics," *Hermeneutics,* Michael Bauman and David W. Hall, eds. (Camp Hill, PA:

Of this civil authority, verse 1 makes it clear, "No authority [exists except] those established by God." The word "establish" is a strong one, meaning "to put in order." Thus, God has ordered the existence of nations, states, and governments. A second time, the end of verse 1 repeats, "The Authorities that exist have been established by God"; therefore, one needs to be very careful before rejecting a government "established by God."

Part of the reason for this was stated clearly at the Reformation by Calvin, who in tumultuous times taught: Any government is better than no government at all. For those living under a difficult regime, that may sound discouraging. However, with human sinfulness being what it is, if there is no government at all, anarchy and chaos will frequently harm human life far more than a less than perfect government. Human governments are necessary, and God has provided for this need. Roaming rule by mob serves neither the interests of the Christian or non-Christian.

Christian Publications, 1995), 41-42, summarizes some of the other linguistic possibilities for Romans 13:1:

> Cranfield stresses that the submission enjoined of believers to the government is not to be equated with "uncritical, blind obedience to the authority's every command." Harrison suspects Paul deliberately avoided the verb "obey" precisely because "a circumstance may arise in which [the believer] must choose between obeying God and obeying men (Act 5:29)." Porter even suggests that the word translated "governing" in the NIV should be interpreted to refer to authorities who are qualitatively superior, in this case with respect to their "justness," though it is not clear if its standard usage allows it to be narrowed quite this much. Allan Boesak, writing at the height of apartheid in South Africa, alleged that the "authority" that has been established by God in Rom. 13:1b refers to a power and not to the government itself. As he puts it, "the . . . words, 'For there is no authority except from God,' do not mean that government comes from God, but rather that the *power*, the authority which the government represents is established by God." From this follows the corollary that "a government has power and authority *because, and only as long as*, it reflects the power and authority given by God" (italics his). In Revelation 13 this is clearly not the prevailing state of affairs. Boesak's observations are grammatically possible, though not demonstrable; they are at least worth pondering.

When tempted to criticize a government, one ought to remember that God has established these, and he does so as an outworking either of his blessing or cursing of a nation. What many fail to consider is that people and nations do not always receive blessing from God's hand. Still, they receive what he has decreed for them and what they deserve.

Accordingly, the Christian will not want to be in the position of rebelling against what God has instituted. There is a strong claim for the state in these verses. If one asks, "what is the role of the state?" in these verses, it is *to be the agent of God to keep civil order*. That is one of the biblical duties of the state—to be the God-ordained order keeper in society. The first role of the state, the ministry of order or justice, is to wield authority—authority to protect citizens and freedoms. That is a proper role for the state. The church and the home—as different spheres of rule—do not, however, have the same prerogatives as the state. Each sphere has some unique duties, abilities, and methods.

Civil governors are given a high compliment when they are assigned the same name as a church officer. In verses 4-5, "he is God's servant" or *deacon* (*diakonos*); later the government servant is called a public functionary (*leitourgos*). It is a high honor to be called a deacon—a servant, ordained for ministry. Such perspective radically transforms the role of government. To be a deacon means that the civil ruler is to serve, specifically to serve God in the area of public order. Civil leaders need to know that they are servants, not Lords (Mt. 20:25). There is one true Sovereign, and all civil servants are his servants—not their own masters. As such, they deserve respect. However, if they should forfeit serving God, then citizens are freed from the duty to honor them.

Thomas Hobbes (1588-1679) is sometimes associated with the rise of modern political science. He wrote an influential book, *Leviathan,* which chronicled the English Civil War of the mid-seventeenth century. However, his more lasting contribution to political science may be his coining of the term, "leviathan," which is often used to depict the government with its far-intrusive tentacles as a monster, a huge smothering sea serpent (cf. Job 41). This work anticipated the modern tendency for governments to absorb all they could, leading one commentator to summarize the Hobbesian influence: "God made the universe, but man made the state; so politics was taken away from theologians and became a matter of empirical investigation."

The Role and Duties of the State

Romans 13 articulates the various major tasks assigned to the state. One should recall that the scope and domain of the state—as a unique order of God—is different from the scope of government assigned to either the home or the church. The tasks which are explicitly mandated in Romans 13 are summarized below.

a. *To govern that which is common to citizens and not discharged to some other God-ordained sphere.*

Three main social spheres are designed by God: family, church, and state. The state is restricted and is not to be an all-expansive leviathan, reaching its tentacles into every possible compartment where the citizen will permit. If one understands the sovereignty of God, one sees that the state has delegated tasks and serves according to his plan; it should be structured accordingly. However, the state must never see itself as sovereign, lest it fall into idolatry. The state is not free to write its own charter, but must bow the knee to the true sovereign Creator of the state. Contrary to some modern ideas, there arc actually very few things which God has ordered the state to do. The state is not charged to perform child-care or to provide economic subsidy to all. It is neither empowered to care for medical procedures nor to prohibit citizens' free use of private property. Some states may do these things, but those areas are not explicitly delegated by God. Nor are states designed to provide for retirement, mental health, education, sponsorship for the arts, job benefits for select groups, nor scientific research (unless it is imperative for common need and benefit). Even though some states take on large portions of these and other works, this assumption also explains why governments are in great debt as they over-reach into these non-assigned areas.

When the state assumes responsibility for non-ordained tasks, two questions should be asked: (1) Has God appointed the government to care for those things? and (2) Is it possible that by allowing government to be so expansive, people surrender more responsibility than is healthy? Have we re-created leviathan? Are we better off with larger and more intrusive government? Some citizens remember times when more responsibility was assigned to individuals and communities; there have been times that communities would do without, if they could not pay for some service.

Helmut Thielicke, who lived through World War II and also saw post-war Germany grow to its statist-orientation, advocated a 'minimal state' in an era of totalitarian expansion. Thielicke warned against the totalitarian state because it "necessarily seeks to penetrate every sphere of life and hence to take over the care of children, the chronically ill, the sick, and the aged." Moreover, "The totalitarian state plays the role of the 'universal father'; attending men with its claims and services from the cradle to the grave, it forces on them the same kind of dependence as is evident in all other spheres of life."[220] The modern age has acquiesced to allow the state to provide many goods and services, whereas earlier God or families were trusted for these. Christians must be on guard against the maximalization by, or the deification of, the state. Thielicke warns that it can be subtle: "This totalitarian or maximal state [acts] as universal father, the state which intervenes in all things, exploiting even the inner powers of man . . . and registering everything and laying claim to everything, transgresses its allotted sphere on the left hand and—whether latently or deliberately—assumes the role of a pseudo church."[221] It is necessary to ask occasionally: What allegiances are Christians pledging in exchange for the state's caretaking? Are Christians giving over parts of biblical duty or trust to the state, instead of to the Creator of the state?

---

[220] Helmut Thielicke, *Theological Ethics: Politics* (Grand Rapids: Eerdmans, 1979), vol. 3, 289.
[221] Ibid., 290.

Later Thielicke argues, "once the state establishes a monopoly in the field of [e. g.,] welfare, once it is forced to render 'complete care for its citizens in body and soul,' it not only reduces individual initiative but also kindles suspicion of the welfare work of other groups." One of the ill-effects is the "universal tendency toward the eradication of the diaconate and its activities,"[222] as the task of welfare is turned over to the maximal state. Thielicke diagnoses the two-step process: "The first phase is the development of the state monopoly. The second is the exclusion of all independent outside actions which seem to dissipate the centrally directed effort and introduce ideologies of their own."[223] Moreover, "How far all this can get from any direct person-to-person care of a fellow human being finally becomes clear in the fact that the burden of the material requirements of state welfare must be borne by general taxation."[224] It is instructive to note that these things were written years ago about truths that have recently been displayed by statist collapses.

Compared with the earlier day, Thielicke sees a stark contrast. In a properly related posture, the minimalist state embraces the church and private charity, "always standing ready to give up tasks as other non-state agents become available. . . . Negatively, this means that the state should oppose the trend toward a total and direct assumption of all welfare tasks, and recognize that in this area too it ought ideally to be a minimal state. Obviously, this ideal arrangement has to be fought for, and the church ought to take the lead in fighting for it."[225]

In conclusion Thielicke stresses,

that the principle of the minimal state derives ultimately from the theological character of the state as an emergency order. This concept contains within itself the postulate that we should commit to the state, not everything we can, but only what we must. It is in keeping with the provisional and interim character of the state that its claims are possible only with the caveat of an ultimate

---

[222] Ibid., 303.
[223] Idem.
[224] Ibid., 301.
[225] Ibid., 312.

> 'Nevertheless.' Where this caveat is omitted, there arises the totalitarian tendency which we have discussed in detail . . . This tendency is accompanied by a similar tendency to level down all distinction, to ignore personal maturity and dignity and to degrade persons to the position of mere objects, and to establish the dominion of the perfected machinery. It was up against this background that we insisted that the state should give up as many tasks as possible and commit them to other agencies. . . . This means that the movement towards totalitarianism will be stemmed only to the degree that non-state agencies actively assume responsibility. The movement will be arrested not by the insight— even the theological insight—of responsible men and groups in government but only by the power of these non-state interceptors, only by men who are prepared to act.[226]

There can only be one Sovereign at a time (Mt. 6:24). If God is not sovereign in a nation, then some other person, agency, or principle will inevitably become sovereign. Sovereignty abhors a vacuum. In all nations, if God is not held Sovereign, another rival— the great governmental Spirit who claims to provide all, the sovereign state—will declare that it can meet needs and is more worthy of worship. One commentator notes: "History has shown that when [belief] comes to its rights, human liberty is assured, while the natural tendency of Atheism is ever towards totalitarianism."[227]

The *minimal* state is much closer to Romans 13 than the maximal state. However, that is not the same as a claim to permit no state. It is better to simply define the state's God-given tasks in terms of merely governing those things of common society not assigned specifically to some other agency.

b. *Punishment of the lawbreakers*. Police are definitely warranted by the state in God's view. Romans 13 speaks of punitive consequences for those who break the law. By rebelling, they bring judgment on themselves (v. 2) and are "terrorized" by rulers (v. 3).

---

[226] Ibid., 316.

[227] Geoffrey Wilson, *Romans: A Digest of Reformed Comment* (Edinburgh: Banner of Truth, 1978), *in loc.*

Law enforcement officers or policemen are needed to restrain, and God did not expect the state to be able to do without them.

Of course, even law enforcement professionals can become corrupt or abuse their position. That is why there are procedural safeguards against that possibility. The state may set up its own law officers to enforce its own laws. If a citizen wants to be free from worry about them, then he must obey the laws. The state is also authorized to make laws, enforce constitutions, and devise order.

c. *Along with this, comes extended authority in areas related to law enforcement.* The state may "bear the sword" (v. 4), symbolizing that the state may use physical punishment on lawbreakers. The phrase "bear the sword" refers at least to capital punishment; the state may take life for heinous crimes. In this case, the state acts as "an agent of wrath" to punish the wrongdoer. There are various punishments, ranging from small to capital. The state may build jails, provide for a legal system that tries and executes the laws of the land, and levy fines. The state is allowed to provide for the whole judicial system and criminal code. Its goal is to protect its citizens. The state is to have that in mind as it acts as a "nurturing parent."

d. Besides the criminal and judicial areas, by extension *the state may "punish the evildoer" if that evildoer is imminently threatening the citizenry; waging a just war punishes the evildoer.* Providing for the common defense is also a legitimate function of government. The state should make sure that it provides only the right kind of defense, an ample one but not necessarily as overwhelming as possible.[228] When a state wages war, it must be careful to keep the interests of its citizens at the forefront and wage a just war. Defense is a God-given area for the state.

e. *Tax* (v. 6). In order to pay for its legitimate expenses and the services of its servants (v. 6), government is allowed to tax in order not to rob. At this point, let me merely plead for two things regarding taxation:

---

[228] Since only God can truly protect us, we may pursue limited degrees of protection without ignoring other moral requirements.

1. The state should not commit to provide things for which it cannot pay through the ordinary tax code (except in true emergencies). If tax revenues cannot pay for something, then it probably should not be undertaken. This imposes a budgetary discipline on administrations that is healthy, and not dissimilar to the budget restrictions expected of other governments, i.e., the home and the church. If taxation cannot provide for some program, states and citizens must question if indebtedness for such activities is warranted by Scripture.

2. The government should not tax at a rate that elevates the state over the importance of God. (Some think a 10% rate should be maximum). *If so many functions did not depend so much on the state, the rate of taxation would not be so high.* One effective way to change tax rates (although requiring a generation) is for Christians to disciple their children and neighbors about the limited role of the state.

In sum, the state can provide order in areas not discharged to others, punish lawbreakers, devise a judicial code and criminal justice system, tax, and provide what is necessary for common defense.

A good guide to what the state may *not* do (according to one earlier statement) is summarized below. The state ought not to: (1) administer the Word or Sacraments; (2) exercise church discipline (nor prevent it when regular); (3) interfere with the church's internal life (WCF 23:3). Yet as 'nursing fathers' the state is to: (1) protect the church's property as any other private property; (2) protect the person and reputation of religious people; (3) insure freedom of worship; and (4) take order that all religious and ecclesiastical assemblies be held without hindrance.

Doug Bandow summarizes the role of limited government as primarily to provide for the believer's right to worship God and to regulate violent or fraudulent interpersonal conduct.[229] He comments:

---

[229] Doug Bandow, *Beyond Good Intentions* (Wheaton: Crossway, 1988), 81-101.

Government has a specific biblical purpose, being ordained by God to regulate relations among men in a fallen world. The functions which Scripture mandates government to perform are few: preserving order, protecting life and property, and maintaining justice and righteousness. At the same time, however, the power of godly government must be limited, and no state can interfere with people's right to worship God. Though government may have a backup role in helping the needy, the primary responsibility for that task lies with individuals. In ancient Israel the Lord relied on the civil authorities to enforce religious law, but that grant of authority appears to have been limited to the covenant nation of Israel.[230]

Robert Dabney summarized the powers of the state as limited to regulating secular rights, equally protecting members of society, taxing, punishing for capital crimes, and waging a defensive war.[231] Dabney wrote, "The object of civil government is simply the protection of temporal rights against aggression, foreign or domestic."[232]

In this century, governments have expanded at an enormous pace. A nation may be in danger of delegating to the state many things that individuals alone or families could be doing. Most modern states have expanded benefits and state-subsidies that most of our grandparents would not have imagined. Some people are even in danger of giving over whole, and important, segments of their lives to Big Brother. Christians may even be gradually yielding responsibilities for the most important things in life—children's education, care for parents, physical health, ministry to the poor, and

---

[230] Ibid., 101. Bandow proceeds to note: "In between the polarities of what is required and what is prohibited lies a large area where our perspectives may be informed by biblical standards, but where we must rely on prudential judgment to evaluate specific policy proposals. In this way our involvement in politics, like our interaction with people in so many other worldly endeavors, requires us to use the wisdom with which God has so graciously offered to endow us."

[231] Robert L. Dabney, *Lectures in Systematic Theology* (rpr. Grand Rapids: Baker, 1985), 869-870. His argument for a defensive war is stated succinctly: "The magistrate who is charged with the sword, to avenge and prevent domestic murder, is *a fortiori* charged to punish and prevent the foreign murderer."

[232] Ibid., 882.

other things—to the providence of the state instead of to the providence of God. Christians who give their greatest allegiance to God must be vigilant about where they place their dependency.

The state has inflated its scope, but it is not merely because of statism—although human beings created in the image of God do have an innate drive to become total sovereigns, if unchecked. Statist expansionism has surfaced not merely because of statist aggressiveness, but also because of Christians' laziness, short-sightedness, unfamiliarity with the whole counsel of God, and unwillingness to carry out some difficult but necessary duties. In many cases, believers have abdicated too much to the government.

In modern times, some states have taken on nearly messianic proportions. Any biblical person must guard against that. Rousas Rushdoony has warned against the state seeking to become Messianic.

> The state as civil government is strictly limited in that, first, it is under God and must administer justice in faithfulness to his word. Second, the state cannot assume as its own those areas which are properly the spheres of the home, school, church, art, economics, or anything else. Third, the state cannot limit the individual's freedom to work out the divine mandate for man as God's image-bearer. Fourth, the authority of the state is at all times ministerial, or delegated from God, not creative or independent.[233]

The Role and Duties of the Christian Citizen

Christians wonder about the tactics of those who break the law as an effort to protect innocent life: "Is it appropriate to protest against a law that is contrary to God's revealed law?" Christians may express their disagreement with laws, and our society protects the right to freely express or protest such matters of conscience. However, Christians have a dual responsibility: they are also to obey the human law, unless to do so is to disobey God. As horrible as the law is that allows for the slaughter of the unborn, still no one in our

---

[233] Rousas J. Rushdoony, *Thy Kingdom Come* (Fairfax, VA: Thoburn Press, 1985), 194.

country is legally compelled to seek an abortion. It would be a different question if a law was passed (e.g., as in China) forbidding its citizens to have as many children as they wanted, with abortion being the mechanism to take that life. If the question is the role of resistance, mandatory abortion is ethically different from permitted abortion.

As long as one stays within the confines to the law, it is permissible to protest or devise other means to seek to change the law. Even if one wants to change the law, that citizen must work within the law to have it changed by constitutional processes. Biblically speaking, one may express disagreement with aspects of a government, but a Christian must be careful to do so peacefully and lawfully. Disciples are not called by God to resort to ungodly methods, even if attempting to correct ungodly parts of our state. The Christian is called to submit to the laws of the state, unless they *mandate* something that is opposite of God's Word.

The same issue can be raised from a different angle. Equally, the state should suppress violence when a mob seeks to prevent a Christian church from having its worship service. In a well-known case, a group of homosexuals protested in front of a church that was hosting a conference on family values, physically preventing worshippers from peacefully attending that service. Sadly the police sat idly by because it was not politically correct in that particular community to restrain homosexuals who expressed their opposition to Christian values. The point is, nevertheless, that the state should protect the freedom to worship as one chooses.

If that is so, then Christians should not be involved in illegally preventing others from having a legal abortion. I reluctantly have to agree. The principle is the same, and if in fairness one expects the state to protect the Christian's civil rights, then he must respect others'—even if they seek something that is self-destructive. Christians should be moved to compassion on behalf of the unborn, but they must make sure that their methods are within the bounds of Scripture. Christians must not resort to unbiblical means, even with a righteous end in sight.

The state is limited and not Messianic in its scope. It is to do only that which God had ordered it to do, and recognize that God has also raised up other groups, like the home, the church, and private charity to take care of many things. The state is to be minimal, not maximal; and it is a creation of God, not human accident—nor even justified solely for administrative efficiency.

It is as important to know what Scripture says about the clear duties of Christians as it is to know the limitations of the state. These duties are clear, but the heart of the problem in this area, as with other areas, is selective rebellion. It is tempting to trumpet the inerrancy of Scripture when one agrees with some portion of Scripture. It is a temptation to love one's country and submit to the government if it is in the hands of one party or one group of leaders. A properly balanced approach follows the Scriptures that prescribe our duties regardless of who rules. Romans 13 aids us in this, too, as it charts our duties.

Duty #1 *is to submit, as long as the government is heeding its proper scope and authority.* Flowing from the earlier God-given authority for the state, the corresponding duty is to submit.

There are few words in modern vocabulary that are more out of favor, especially in America. Submission is not the favorite past-time of Americans, nor a virtue quickly associated with our people. Children do not enjoy it, teenagers hate it, and adults may like it less. Yet, the unbending reality is that God has created the world with certain inbuilt structures that can neither be avoided or ignored. He calls Christians to submit to those things which he has made. But rebellious sinners, do not like this and do not want to obey.

* Wives do not want to submit to their husbands *by nature.*

* Children do not want to submit to their parents *by nature.*

* Employees do not want to submit to their employers *by nature.*

* Church members do not want to submit to their elders *by nature.*

* Citizens do not want to submit to their civil rulers *by nature.*

Following Adam, by nature people all want to be Sovereigns. We lust to be king; if permitted we choose to enthrone ourselves and seek to erect our own petty fiefdoms—*by nature.*

Submission is difficult, and sinful human nature does not enjoy subordination.[234] It requires a maturity of perspective, a heart that knows God's ways of working are larger than man's ways, the fruit of the spirit, and a deep trust that God's ways are best. Submission is directly and ultimately tied to the amount of trust in God. If a person can accept that God is precisely as described in Scripture, and that he acts precisely as Scripture describes, then one can submit.

It is helpful to recall that this passage in Romans was not written merely to apply to modern democracies. It was written during the rule of emperors like Nero, a cruel opponent of Christianity. How a Christian can possibly submit to such manifest tyranny and oppression is only possible if one understands who God is and what he does. It is only as one truly believes that God is the real Sovereign and that he is actively working out his plan that one can submit to less than perfect governments.

Proper submission is a teaching of God's whole counsel, and one cannot circumvent it by changing the meaning of the term. It was originally a military term, and most literally means "to fall into rank," indicating that God has certain places, certain ranks, and certain orders to be observed. All people are not called to the same place of service. It is sinful to try to overthrow those orders that God has created, *assuming* that our authorities are God ordained. God is a God of order, not anarchy. Unless the governors have ceased to fit in with God's order (forfeiture), then to rebel against them is to rebel against God.

1 Peter 2:13 ff. reaffirms, "Submit yourselves for the Lord's sake to every authority instituted among men: whether to the king, as supreme authority, or to governors, who are sent by him to punish those who do wrong and to commend those who do right."

---

[234] While John Yoder is correct to note that the command in Romans 13:1 employs a different word than the New Testament word for obedience, notwithstanding, the call for submission entails a large measure of obedience; else the concept would be totally frustrated. More correctly, Yoder does recognize that even the resister who rejects the government's immoral commands, "still remains under the sovereignty of that government and accepts the penalties which it imposes . . . the Christian . . . is being subordinate even though not obeying." John H. Yoder, *The Politics of Jesus* (2nd ed., Grand Rapids: Eerdmans, 1994), 209.

Obedience in this area is one way of silencing critics and spreading the gospel according to that chapter (v. 15). The paragraph concludes: "Show proper respect to everyone; Love the brotherhood of believers, fear God, honor the king." It is not, therefore, only Romans 13 that teaches this, but the consistent biblical witness.

The complex issue is: "When does the Christian *not* submit to the state? Or is the Christian universally, categorically in every instance to submit to the state, such that to rebel against the state is always to sin against God?"

Consider that first question first. We have already noted instances in which believers did not obey the state. In Exodus 1, Pharaoh ordered the midwives to kill male children when born. They disobeyed and fabricated a half-true excuse. Nevertheless, God approved of the midwives disobeying in that instance. Saints disobeyed and were blessed for it. Obadiah is commended (1 Kgs. 18:4) for sheltering 100 true prophets in contravention to the Queen's direct order to murder them. In Acts 4, when the Sanhedrin ordered the apostles not to preach the gospel, authorities attempted to outlaw evangelism. Peter responded, "Judge for yourselves whether it is right in God's sight to obey you rather than God. For we cannot help speaking about what we have seen and heard." Hence, the disciples did not stop preaching, and God mightily blessed the church.

Other biblical teachings outside of Romans 13 convey that there are times when Christians do not obey the civil government due to higher allegiance to a higher power. There are some times—should the government explicitly and unavoidably order the breaking of God's law—that believers have to obey God and not man. In those cases, submission is morally wrong. That is not to contradict what it is written in Romans 13; it is merely to harmonize Romans 13 with other clear teachings of Scripture. It is allowing Scripture to interpret Scripture.

Notice that resistance is acceptable only after:
* *all other measures and appeals have been made;*
* *when it is an overt mandate to break a definite teaching;*
* *adoption of willful agreement to suffer legal consequence.*

In qualified cases, Christians are justified in not obeying the illegitimate government, because that government forfeits the right to be obeyed. If civil law breaks God's law, Christians will not be able to obey.

The doctrine of forfeiture maintains that it is *normally* the Christian duty to submit to God-ordained authorities. However, if authorities blatantly transgress the parameters God has established for them—if they move outside of their lawful authority as designed by God—then they forfeit the right to submission.[235] In these cases, it is not the obedient Christian who sins when they do not submit to the authority, but the authority who sins by encroaching another's domain. When the civil ruler does this, he forfeits his claim on the life of citizens. To command disobedience to God, requires the Christian to resist. Robert Dabney stated, "If the thing commanded by the civil magistrate is positively sinful, then the Christian citizen must refuse obedience, but yield submission to the penalty therefore."[236] While arguing against indefinite passive obedience to an evil form of government, he also remarked: "God has not ordained what government mankind shall live under, but only that they shall live under a government. . . . When a form of government entirely ceases, as a whole, to subserve its proper end, is it still to subsist forever? This is preposterous. . . . The meaning of the apostle is, that this resistance must be the act, not of the individual, but of the people. The insubordination which he condemns, is that which

---

[235] Theodore Beza articulated this idea: "if anyone strives to seize or has already usurped an unjust tyranny over others, whether he be a stranger or whether as a viper he leaps from the womb of his country . . . then shall private citizens . . . approach their legitimate magistrates in order that . . . the public enemy be cast forth by the public authority and common consent of all. But if the magistrate connives (at the attempt) or in some way refuses to perform his duty, then let each private citizen bestir himself with all his power to defend the lawful constitution of his country, to whom after God he owes his entire existence, against him who cannot be deemed a lawful magistrate since he either has already usurped that rank in violation of the public laws or is endeavoring to usurp it." Theodore Beza, *Concerning the Rights of Rulers over Their Subjects and the Duty of Subjects Towards Their Rulers*, Henry-Louis Gonin, trans.; Patrick S. Poole, ed., *Reformation Political Tracts* (forthcoming), Question 4.

[236] Dabney, op. cit., 870.

arrays against a bad government . . . the worse anarchy of the individual will."[237]

Johannes Althusius articulated the doctrine of forfeiture well. He noted that rulers were "not permitted to overstep these [constitutional] limits. Those who exceed the boundaries of administration entrusted to them cease being ministers of God and . . . become private persons to whom obedience is not owed in those things in which they exceed the limits of their power."[238] Furthermore, he defined the types of situations in which forfeiture was clear. Rulers forfeited their legitimate claim to obedience when: (1) they mandate "something to be done that is prohibited by God in the first table of the Decalogue, or to be omitted that is therein prescribed by God"; (2) they prohibit "something that cannot be omitted, or command something that cannot be committed, without violating holy charity"; or (3) they "seek their personal and private benefit rather than the common utility and welfare" of the nation.[239]

In the well-known life-story of Corrie Ten Boom, many are acquainted with how she and her family worked to shelter Jewish people as part of the Dutch Resistance movement in WWII. The state had ordered all people of Jewish heritage to be killed, simply because of their ethnic background. Moreover, citizens were required to turn them over to officers of the state, and citizens knew they were handing over people to be slaughtered. In essence, the state was commanding these citizens to break the sixth commandment, and Christians owed a higher allegiance to God than to a wicked state; thus they resisted. Had the government not required direct participation in murder, Christians could have submitted. Christians are called to obey the state, even if it is less than perfect. Christians disobey it, only when it reaches a point of corruption such that it legislates in opposition to God.

Specific governments may forfeit their charter. They are set up to obey God. If they consistently and willfully disobey God, they may reach a point at which Christians cannot obey. Corrie Ten Boom and

---

[237] Ibid., 872.

[238] Johannes Althusius, *Politica* (Indianapolis: Liberty Fund, 1995), 98.

[239] Ibid., 98.

others are good examples of keeping the state under God and serving God first.

The same is true in any relationship of submission. A superior may forfeit the right to have obedience, if he directly opposes God. Those in positions of authority must remember that they serve God and not themselves. They are not licensed to do anything they wish, but to serve the wishes of God. If they abandon that charter, they lose their license. In these cases, to invoke forfeiture there must be a case of actual violation of God's standards, not merely legislation that one does not especially prefer.

In all the cases above, the superior should not be obeyed, for to do so would be to sin against God. Submission is limited by responsibility to the Divine. Nevertheless, as long as the government is not contradicting God, then Christians must submit.

Later in Romans 13, there are two reasons given (v. 5) for submitting to the law: (1) because of possible punishment—pragmatically to keep Christians from squandering their time and resources in criminal sentences, and (2) for conscience sake. That is, to keep our consciences from being guilty, we should obey the law, lest we have to continually look over our shoulders wondering if the authorities will catch us.

Duty #2: *Pay taxes*. The command in Scripture is clear that the civil ruler can require the payment of taxes. These are civil funds, and not to be confused with the tithe which belongs uniquely to the church. Revenue is also permissible. Revenue is slightly different from taxes; more like user-fees or custom payments. In one sense they are all taxes, but revenue differs slightly from taxes in that services rendered are more immediate for revenues. In Scripture (and most ancient cultures), rates of taxation or revenue were equal rates or equal amounts.

Duty #3: *Respect*. Sometimes it is difficult for Christians to give respect; it is a responsibility that should not be shirked, regardless of the leaders in office. Christians should not despise God's work by disrespecting those God has given over them. Respect should be given to those in positions of leadership.

Duty #4: *Honor.* This is the same word used for "honor your father and mother." The use of this word nuances this duty. Christians are summoned to honor civil leaders like parents. Christians should look for ways to build them up and give them proper praise, support, and encouragement.

Let me hasten to add one final duty to the list from 1 Timothy 2.

Duty #5: *Pray for authorities.* The clear command of 1 Timothy 2 is to pray for all those in authority with the goal being freedom to lead unhindered Christian lives. From time to time, some Christians believe that a particular administration may be the most vile in all history. Admittedly, in any country, there are some good regimes and some poor ones. Some are closer to God's Word, and therefore easier to pray for, while others are clearly far away from God's statutes.

It is no question that the Christian has a duty to pray for our leaders. But *what* do we pray for them? For example, should Christians pray for them to repent and come to their senses? Sometimes that is appropriate and there is biblical precedent for that in the Psalms. Other times, there are examples in the Bible of outright opposition. That is to say, on some occasions in Scripture, believers pray directly *against* the governors, and pray for their destruction and judgment. Those are severe prayers, but one must not overlook the fact that the inspired Hymnbook (the Psalms) contains an entire category of prayer-songs that invoke God's judgment on rulers who oppose him. Evidently, that is acceptable to God at times, else it would certainly have been stricken from the Bible.

To make the point even more directly, not only is it merely permissible to God—for believers at times to pray against wicked rulers (instead of acts of rebellion)—but it is also a pattern of response that Christians in post-biblical times could employ. If, as this Scripture teaches, the Christian is not to break the law unless imperatively commanded by the civil law to break God's higher law, and still that government remains intractably wicked, if one cannot resort to physical acts, God does not merely instruct believers to become pacifists. Instead, he gives another whole arsenal of weapons, a spiritual set of tools. Prayer is chief among them. If a ruler consistently and adamantly rules contrary to God's Word, then it may be that Christians must pray for God's judgment to come quickly to wipe away that blot from society.

Yet, praying for God's judgment to descend on people is a very difficult thing to do, and must be applied with the greatest of care. The Christian's main desire is to see people come to Christ—not to be destroyed. One should be careful about praying for God's judgment, but on the other hand, that may be appropriate in some cases.

In the first centuries after Christ, when Christians were under persecution, grandparents in the faith prayed regularly for the political rulers. When Paul wrote Romans 13, the exceedingly cruel emperor was Nero, who only a few years later would persecute Christians. If Paul and others in the first centuries AD could practice and preach submission to evil governments, then how can we do less? Most situations hardly parallel actual persecution. Early Christians left behind a clear tradition of praying for political leaders.

Justin Martyr (ca. AD 150 in *Apology* 1:17) wrote: "And everywhere, we, more readily than all men, endeavor to pay those appointed by you the taxes, both ordinary and extraordinary, as we have been taught by him . . . Whence to God alone we render worship, but in other things we will gladly serve you, acknowledging you as kings and rulers of men, and praying that with your kingly power you may be found to possess also sound judgment. But if you pay no regard to our prayers and frank explanations, we shall suffer no loss, since we believe . . . that every man will suffer punishment in eternal fire according to the merit of his deed, and will render account according to the power he has received from God . . ."[240]

---

[240] Justin Martyr, "First Apology," *Ante-Nicene Fathers*, Alexander Roberts and James Donaldson, eds. (1885, rpr. Peabody, MA: Hendrickson Publishers, 1995), vol. 1, 168. In Justin Martyr's "The Sole Government of God," (Ibid., 290-293), the early apologist compiles various pre-Christian poets' comments on God as administrator (governor) of the universe to refute idolatry.

Once while pleading for peace, Athenagoras, another early Christian teacher and writer, stated: "We deserve favor because we pray for your government, that you may, as is most equitable, receive increase and addition, until all men become subject to your sway."[241]

Tertullian (*Apology* 30, ca. AD 200) reported:

We offer prayer for the safety of our princes to the eternal, the true, the living God, whose favor beyond all other things, they must themselves desire. They know from whom they have obtained their power . . . They reflect upon the extent of their power and so they come to understand the highest; they acknowledge that they have all their might from him against whom their might is nought. Let the emperor make war on heaven; let him lead heaven captive in his triumph; let him put guards on heaven; let him impose taxes on heaven! He cannot. . . . He gets his scepter where he first got his humanity; his power where he got the breath of life. . . . Without ceasing, for all our emperors we offer prayer. We pray for life prolonged; for security to the empire; for protection for the imperial house; for brave armies, a faithful senate, a virtuous people, the world at rest—whatever, as man or Caesar, and emperor would wish. . . [because the emperor] is called by our Lord to his office. . . on valid grounds I might say **Caesar is more ours than yours** because our God appointed him. Therefore, as having this propriety in him, I do more than you for his welfare, not merely because I ask of him who can give it, or because I ask it as one who deserves to get it, but also because, in keeping the majesty of Caesar within due limits, and putting it under the Most High, and making it less than divine, I commend him the more to the favor of Deity, to whom I make him alone inferior. But I place him in subjection to one I regard as more glorious than himself.[242]

---

[241] Cited by William Barclay, *Daily Study Bible (Romans)* (Philadelphia: Westminster, 1971) *in loc.*

[242] Tertullian, "Apology," *Ante-Nicene Fathers*, Alexander Roberts and James Donaldson, eds. (1885, rpr. Peabody, MA: Hendrickson Publishers, 1995), vol. 3, 42-43.

Such sentiments are both challenging and insightful for our times. If Christians see the civil governor as his own person, truly operating outside the influence and sovereignty of God, then they may have an extremely difficult time praying for him. However, if believers recall what the Scriptures teach—that God is at work, that he is planning out all things for his own glory, that he is raising up and tearing down nations and kings as the grass withers and is thrown into the air, that there is a spiritual plane of reality that is more powerful than even the physical politics—then Christians can affirm with Tertullian that the civil rulers are more ours than others' because God is truly the one who raises them up for his own purposes.

Clement of Rome even offered this prayer which illuminates a proper attitude toward civil authority: "Grant to them, Lord, health, peace, concord, and stability, so that they may exercise without offense the sovereignty that you have given them. Master, heavenly King of the ages, you give glory, honor, and power over the things of earth to the sons of men. Direct, Lord, their counsel, following what is pleasing and acceptable in your sight, so that by exercising with devotion and in peace and gentleness the power that you have given to them, they may find favor with you."[243]

The earlier doctrines in the epistle to the Romans are essential for a right understanding of Romans 13. These verses would not make sense if introduced first apart from the Sovereignty of God or if stripped from their context. In these verses, those earlier teachings on the sole kingship of Christ are further developed. In accord with that, Christ himself raises up certain servants. Some of them are vessels pre-fitted for destruction (cf. Rom. 9), but it is still God who creates them and raises them up. That applies to political leaders—not just in our country, but throughout the world. Similarly, God raises up others who serve him in righteousness and who are to be thanked. In either case, Christians are to submit to these rulers—*unless* they forfeit their right to rule by directly breaking God's law and compelling others to do so. We are to submit, and honor, pray

---

[243] *Catechism of the Catholic Church* (Liguori, MO: Liguori Publications, 1995), 463.

for, and pay for appropriate government. In all of this, the obedient Christian is summoned to submit to God's rule, whether they care for the human instrument of that state or not. The rightly ordered state is intended by God to be a gift for his people. And prayer for governors should not be neglected.

Many believers grow frustrated that the public square is not quickly repaired; admittedly, this is a large and multi-generational project. We also did not devolve into our problems quickly; neither will we necessarily resurface from serious structural problems too quickly. Nevertheless, Christians are called to practice what we preach: reliance on the sovereignty of God over the machinations of man or party, and a steady trust in the tools that God gives—prayer, his Word, and the sacraments—over confidence in princes, armies, or undeliberated quick fixes.

While each Christian may not be called to hold office, vote on legislation, or lobby, every Christian has at least two spheres of lasting influence: in the home and in the church. *First*, in one's home, one may carry out thoughtful discussions, disciple and mentor other family members and friends, and seek to carry that small precinct for the candidate of choice. There is no reason to abdicate the home; nor should individuals as citizens be gagged. *Second*, in one's church—though we do not recommend endorsements or simplistic voters' guides (which always contain their own biases)—believers are called specifically: (1) to pass on to the next generation the faithful teachings of Scripture (2 Tim. 2:2) as they bear on political ideas, (2) to teach and disciple the youth as we journey through life (Dt. 6:1-5), and (3) to teach all things that Christ has commanded (Mt. 28:18-20). If we are also (4) to "take every thought captive" unto the obedience of Christ (2 Cor. 10:5), we must strike the balance between the view of James Thornwell and others, who made it clear that the mission and thrust of the church should never be confused with political activism,[244]

---

[244] Two fine recent works clarifying this point are Michael Horton, *The Gospel Commission: Recovering God's Strategy for Making Disciples* (Grand Rapids: Baker Books, 2011) and Kevin DeYoung, *What is the Mission of the Church? Making Sense of Social Justice, Shalom, and the Great Commission* (Wheaton:

and Abraham Kuyper, who taught that there is not a single inch of the universe, over which King Jesus did not claim, "Mine!"

That mature and balanced posture might lead to many other questions. Questioning politics, however, is not bad. Nor is it wrong to question the prevailing world-spirit or even the dogmas of a conservative party or a liberal party. We may learn much by asking the hard questions. What is even more promising, though, than merely questioning is to find answers that are sound, intransient, and more enduring than the enfeebled opinions of a few individuals, yesterday's elite, or the agendas of a partisan caucus. Wisdom greater than our own is inevitably needed for that. Thankfully, God has not been silent on the most important matters of life. Politics is certainly one of those.

Crossway, 2011).

About the Author

Dr. David W. Hall has served as the Senior Pastor of the historic Midway Presbyterian Church (PCA) in Powder Springs, Georgia since 2003. Previously, he served as Pastor of the Covenant Presbyterian Church in Oak Ridge, Tennessee (1984-2003) and as Associate Pastor at the First Presbyterian Church in Rome, Georgia (1980-1984).

Dr. Hall's undergraduate degree from the University of Memphis (B. A., 1975) was in philosophy. After completion of his undergraduate studies, Pastor Hall studied at Swiss L'Abri and then enrolled at Covenant Theological Seminary in St. Louis, Missouri, graduating in 1980. He later earned a Ph.D. in Christian Intellectual Thought from Whitefield Theological Seminary.

In addition to pastoring, David Hall is the author or editor of over 20 books and numerous essays. He was also the Founder and Senior Fellow of the Kuyper Institute in Oak Ridge, Tennessee. In addition to his commentaries and *Kuyper Institute Briefings*, his works include: *The Genevan Reformation and the American Founding; Savior or Servant? Putting Government in Its Place; Election Day Sermons; The Arrogance of the Modern: Historical Theology Held in Contempt; Holding Fast to Creation; The Millennium of Jesus Christ: An Exposition of* The Revelation *for All Ages, Welfare Reformed: A Compassionate Approach* and *A Heart Promptly Offered: The Revolutionary Leadership of John Calvin.*

In addition to his work as Executive Director of Calvin500, his Calvin500 series contains the following works: *The Legacy of John Calvin, Calvin in the Public Square, Calvin and Commerce, Preaching Like Calvin, Calvin and Culture, Tributes to John Calvin,* and *Theological Guide to Calvin's* Institutes.

Other Kindle e-books by the author may be found at:
http://www.amazon.com/David-W.-Hall/e/B001HPPL7E/ref=ntt_dp_epwbk_0

For titles that may be obtained by contacting the author directly for a discount, email: david.hall@midwaypca.org.

Or consult the author's Amazon.com page at:
http://www.amazon.com/gp/search/ref=sr_tc_2_0?rh=i%3Astripbooks%2Ck%3ADavid+W.+Hall&keywords=David+W.+Hall&ie=UTF8&qid=1318280819&sr=1-2-ent&field-contributor_id=B001HPPL7E#/ref=sr_pg_2?rh=n%3A283155%2Ck%3ADavid+W.+Hall%2Cp_82%3AB001HPPL7E&page=2&keywords=David+W.+Hall&ie=UTF8&qid=1318280828